Who Said That?

A PRACTICAL GUIDE TO HEARING AND FEELING GOD FOR YOURSELF

Tiffany Downs

Copyright © 2019 by Tiffany Downs

Who Said That?

All rights reserved. No part of this publication may be reproduced, distributed or transmitted in any form or by any means, including photocopying, recording, or other electronic or mechanical methods, without the prior written permission of the publisher, except in the case of brief quotations embodied in critical reviews and certain other noncommercial uses permitted by copyright law.

Although the author and publisher have made every effort to ensure that the information in this book was correct at press time, the author and publisher do not assume and hereby disclaim any liability to any party for any loss, damage, or disruption caused by errors or omissions, whether such errors or omissions result from negligence, accident, or any other cause.

Adherence to all applicable laws and regulations, including international, federal, state and local governing professional licensing, business practices, advertising, and all other aspects of doing business in the US, Canada or any other jurisdiction is the sole responsibility of the reader and consumer.
Neither the author nor the publisher assumes any responsibility or liability whatsoever on behalf of the consumer or reader of this material. Any perceived slight of any individual or organization is purely unintentional.

The resources in this book are provided for informational purposes only and should not be used to replace the specialized training and professional judgment of a health care or mental health care professional.

Neither the author nor the publisher can be held responsible for the use of the information provided within this book. Please always consult a trained professional before making any decision regarding treatment of yourself or others.

Copyright Notices

Unless otherwise indicated, all Scripture quotations are taken from the Holy Bible, New Living Translation, copyright © 1996, 2004, 2015 by Tyndale House Foundation. Used by permission of Tyndale House Publishers, Inc., Carol Stream, Illinois 60188. All rights reserved.

Scripture quotations marked CSB have been taken from the Christian Standard Bible ®, Copyright © 2017 by Holman Bible Publishers. Used by permission. Christian Standard Bible ® and CSB ® are federally registered trademarks of Holman Bible Publishers.

Scripture quotations marked ESV are from the ESV® Bible (The Holy Bible, English Standard Version®), copyright © 2001 by Crossway, a publishing ministry of Good News Publishers. Used by permission. All rights reserved.

Scripture quotations marked NIV have been taken from The Holy Bible, New International Version® NIV® Copyright © 1973, 1978, 1984, 2011 by Biblica, Inc.™ Used by permission. All rights reserved worldwide.

Scripture marked NKJV has been taken from the New King James Version ®, Copyright © 1982 by Thomas Nelson. Used by Permission. All rights reserved.

Scripture quotations marked TPT are from The Passion Translation®. Copyright ©2017, 2018 by Passion & Fire Ministries, Inc. Used by permission. All rights reserved. ThePassionTranslation.com.

Book Layout ©2017 BookDesignTemplates.com

Ordering Information:
Quantity sales. Special discounts are available on quantity purchases by corporations, associations, and others. For details, contact the "Special Sales Department" at the address above.

Who Said That?/Tiffany Downs. —1st ed.
ISBN 978-1-952015-00-7 (e-book)
ISBN 978-1-952015-01-4 (paperback)

Dedication

This book is dedicated to my mom, Sherry, beloved member of the cloud of witnesses. This is your legacy.

Dear friends,

What an honor to write the foreword to the book you are holding in your hands or reading electronically, authored by my sweet friend, Tiffany. Within moments you will be connected to the God of the universe as she shares her personal story and invites you to join her in prayers that express the longing of one's heart to see and hear Him. With vivid pictures, Tiffany weaves together the beautiful threads of the Father's heart plan—the redemption story of Jesus from the prophets to Revelation. She introduces us to the Holy Spirit who reveals truth, guides, and empowers us in a very intimate and personal way. This is no mere "how to" book on hearing the voice of God, but rich revelation of the Godhead—Father, Son, and Holy Spirit who are continually speaking and listening to one another desiring for mankind to enter the conversations of heaven. May your life never be the same as you hear the affirming words of agape love! May you carry His heart mission to reach others that they, too, may hear His voice.

Pastor Dee Mueller
Hearth Ministries

Contents

Hearing God's Voice 1
    My First Time 3
He Is the Lamb of God 11
"He Existed Long Before Me" 29
Baptism 35
"The Spirit Will Tell You" 43
Why Is the Holy Spirit Important? 53
    Fan into Flame 55
    Quenching the Fire 57
Where Do You Bubble? 67
Practice: Asking Questions and the Holy Spirit Game .. 83
The Rest of My Story 95
Relationship with Jesus 121
Resources 125
About the Author 131

CHAPTER 1

Hearing God's Voice

You can picture it, can't you? A deep, booming voice accompanied by a shaft of light illuminating my face as I kneel before God. His hands gently lifting my chin so my eyes can rest upon his face. I feel like the only person in the world, and I have his full attention. Boy, that's a great place to be!

I'd love to tell you this was my first encounter with hearing God, but in all honesty I can't. It almost seems real because I can see it so clearly. Imaginably this was happening in my spirit. God does speak to people like this. The first time I heard him speak convinced me beyond a shadow of a doubt it was his voice. Nobody can take that from me.

I want you to have this same assurance for yourself. I'm willing to bet you already hear God. I believe he is using this book to show you he has been speaking to you all these years. God wants you to be confident you hear his voice *every day*. Would you pray with me?

> *God, you have made yourself so accessible to us. The veil is torn[1] and we now have the ability to communicate with you and you with us. Would you open our eyes and ears,[2] Lord? I pray over those reading this now. Heal their hearts from*

---

1. "But the people's minds were hardened, and to this day whenever the old covenant is being read, the same veil covers their minds so they cannot understand the truth. And this veil can be removed only by believing in Christ. Yes, even today when they read Moses' writings, their hearts are covered with that veil, and they do not understand. But whenever someone turns to the Lord, the veil is taken away. For the Lord is the Spirit, and wherever the Spirit of the Lord is, there is freedom. So all of us who have had that veil removed can see and reflect the glory of the Lord. And the Lord—who is the Spirit—makes us more and more like him as we are changed into his glorious image" (2 Corinthians 3:14–18).
2. "Look, a righteous king is coming! And honest princes will rule under him. Each one will be like a shelter from the wind and a refuge from the storm, like streams of water in the desert and the shadow of a great rock in a parched land. Then everyone who has eyes will be able to see the truth, and everyone who has ears will be able to hear it" (Isaiah 32:1–3).

religion and lies that say you are distant and no longer speak.[3] *Thank you for desiring this for us. If only we could realize how much you say and how much we are missing! Oh God, please allow us to catch just a little more than what we've already heard you speaking over us. Open our ears to the songs you sing.*[4] *Thank you for what you are doing through this book and in the lives of every person praying with me. Just a little more, in the name of Jesus.*

My First Time

Nearly twenty-five years ago, a single moment changed my life forever.

---

3. "The Lord is close to all who call on him, yes, to all who call on him in truth" (Psalm 145:18).
4. "For the Lord your God is living among you. He is a mighty savior. He will take delight in you with gladness. With his love, he will calm all your fears. He will rejoice over you with joyful songs" (Zephaniah 3:17).

The white church van pulled onto the dusty road leading to our trailer park filled with mobile homes. Standing at the end of the driveway, I anticipated this service. I was also glad to leave the house for a while.

I quickly shifted my thoughts to the order of service. I knew the routine by now and found much comfort in this predictable event. In Sunday school, we recited our memory verse and discussed a new story and verse for the following week. How I loved reciting Scripture from memory!

Afterward, everyone gathered in the sanctuary for "big church." That's what we called it anyway. We opened the hymnal for worship. The little old lady behind me began to sing. To my ears, her voice sounded higher-pitched than anyone else's. We were taught God was the most high, so I imagined this woman was pretty close to him. For me, it just wasn't worship without her.

Brother Steve,[5] an old Baptist preacher in southern Georgia, filled the pulpit again. He gave a riveting

---

5. Names have been changed for privacy purposes (and sometimes I

message of which I cannot recall a single word. A tired little girl sitting alone in the pew, I struggled to stay awake. Things move slower in the South, especially lips. A southern drawl is like a lullaby for little ears and tired eyes.

Finally, the altar call. It happened week after week, but something was different during *this* altar call. At the end of service for the past few weeks, I felt a strange sensation in my belly. It felt like a "tug" or "pull." This was different from anything I'd experienced before.

Brother Steve began his closing remarks. "If you need a dad, God wants to be that for you. He is the best daddy you could ever have." My dad lived two states and many hours away. I desperately wanted a dad I could talk to, hug, kiss, and play with anytime. One to share in my activities. *I'm listening now! Tell me more, Brother Steve.* He said God would always be there with me. He would love me more than any earthly dad ever could.

---

couldn't remember!).

I was sold at "He'll be your daddy if you need one." *Why yes, yes. I could use another daddy!* Brother Steve also described this tugging in my belly. He used my words! He said if I felt a tugging inside me, it was *God speaking to me.* I was already sold on God being my daddy, Lord, and Savior. Now there was proof he spoke to me. It doesn't get any better than this. I was done. Down the aisle I went and asked Jesus to come into my heart forever.

I never told anyone about God speaking to me. Honestly, I thought everyone in the church knew he spoke to us. I believe every person can hear God as well as have meaningful conversations with him, speaking to each other as friends just as he did with Moses.[6] Because Jesus died on the cross and rose from the dead three days later, we have direct access to Daddy God.[7] There is no

---

6. "Inside the Tent of Meeting, the Lord would speak to Moses face to face, as one speaks to a friend. Afterward Moses would return to the camp, but the young man who assisted him, Joshua son of Nun, would remain behind in the Tent of Meeting" (Exodus 33:11).
7. "And as Moses lifted up the bronze snake on a pole in the wilderness, so the Son of Man must be lifted up, so that everyone who believes in him will have eternal life. For this is how God loved the world: He gave his one and only Son, so that everyone who believes in him will not perish but have eternal life. God sent his Son into the world not to judge the world, but to save the world

other way.[8] This is how much he desires a relationship with *you*!

C.S. Lewis wrote, "Look for Christ and you will find Him, and with Him everything else thrown in."[9] Having this in mind changes the way you look at the world around yourself and your circumstances. In other words, if you look for Jesus in everything, you will find him.[10] (If you don't know Jesus and would like to begin that relationship, or long ago you were friends, but need to reconnect, let me introduce you. See the appendices for more information and some helpful resources.)

When you finish this book, I hope you will see and hear God in ways you never imagined. My prayer as we continue this journey:

---

through him" (John 3:14–17).
8. "Jesus told him, 'I am the way, the truth, and the life. No one can come to the Father except through me'" (John 14:6).
9. C.S. Lewis, *Mere Christianity* (New York: Macmillan Publishing Company, 1952), p. 190.
10. "God created everything through him, and nothing was created except through him" (John 1:3).

> *Lord, you alone bring understanding and revelation. We cannot create it on our own. We are seeking to know you more, understand you, and see your face. You are always speaking. Thank you for hearing our prayers.*[11] *Anoint the eyes of those reading these words to see. Gift them with ears to hear. Please multiply opportunities to practice hearing your voice and developing deeper friendship with you in the name of Jesus. Thank you for hearing my prayer.*

"Elisha prayed, 'Open his eyes, Lord, so that he may see.' Then the Lord opened the servant's eyes, and he looked and saw the hills full of horses and chariots of fire all around Elisha" (2 Kings 6:17, NIV). This is my prayer for all of you. I also pray you would be like Moses whom God spoke to as a friend, face-to-face. I

---

11. "I have written this to you who believe in the name of the Son of God, so that you may know you have eternal life. And we are confident that he hears us whenever we ask for anything that pleases him. And since we know he hears us when we make our requests, we also know that he will give us what we ask for" (1 John 5:13–15).

pray your relationship with God would go deeper than ever before as you hear him and obey. Jesus said, "I no longer call you servants, because a servant does not know his master's business. Instead, I have called you friends, for everything that I learned from my Father I have made known to you" (John 15:15).

CHAPTER 2

He Is the Lamb of God

Our primary example of how to begin life with Christ is Christ. Let's review how Jesus was first revealed to the world in John 1:26–34:

> John told them, "I baptize with water, but right here in the crowd is someone you do not recognize. Though his ministry follows mine, I'm not even worthy to be his slave and untie the straps of his sandal."
>
> This encounter took place in Bethany, an area east of the Jordan River, where John was baptizing.

The next day John saw Jesus coming toward him and said, "Look! The Lamb of God who takes away the sin of the world! He is the one I was talking about when I said, 'A man is coming after me who is far greater than I am, for he existed long before me.' I did not recognize him as the Messiah, but I have been baptizing with water so that he might be revealed to Israel."

Then John testified, "I saw the Holy Spirit descending like a dove from heaven and resting upon him. I didn't know he was the one, but when God sent me to baptize with water, he told me, 'The one on whom you see the Spirit descend and rest is the one who will baptize with the Holy Spirit.' I saw this happen to Jesus, so I testify that he is the Chosen One of God."

In this passage, religious leaders interviewed John. They compared his testimony against Scripture. The Jewish leaders meticulously studied the scrolls because they were looking for the Messiah. They memorized passages equivalent to our books of the Bible. They analyzed hundreds of statements their ancestral prophets spoke looking for the Messiah in every word.

In the above Scripture passage, God reveals three important facts about Jesus: 1) He is the Lamb of God who takes away the sin of the world; 2) He existed long before John; and 3) Jesus, the Chosen One of God, would baptize with the Holy Spirit.

Let's dig deep into Scripture and first explore Jesus as the Lamb of God. If you haven't noticed, I like to ask questions. My first question is, "Why the Lamb of God?" Why not something else? There are other references to Jesus as the Lion of Judah.[1] So why a lamb? A baby sheep to be exact. Let's start at the beginning of Scripture.

---

1. "But one of the twenty-four elders said to me, 'Stop weeping! Look, the Lion of the tribe of Judah, the heir to David's throne, has won the victory. He is worthy to open the scroll and its seven seals'" (Revelation 5:5).

The first instance of slaughtering a lamb other than for eating occurs during the Passover in Exodus 12. God told his people he was going to kill the firstborn son of every living being in the land. He gave the Israelites detailed instructions on how to avoid the consequences of this plague.[2] The fathers were to slaughter a lamb, drain its blood, and brush the blood across the top and sides of their doorframes with a hyssop branch.[3] The motion of their hands may create a cross in the air. One could argue this directly points to Jesus whose blood was painted on a cross as he was crucified. God "passed over" the families who obeyed him by putting the blood of the lamb on their door posts.

Why is this important? What does this have to do with Jesus and hearing God's voice? Would you believe me if I said *everything*? The lamb was such an important part of Passover. God went to great lengths to orchestrate the most important event in human history at Passover:

---

2. Exodus 12 has specific instructions on how to prepare the lamb, what to do with its blood, and even what to wear while eating the lamb.
3. "They are to take some of the blood and smear it on the sides and top of the doorframes of the houses where they eat the animal" (Exodus 12:7).

Jesus's death and resurrection.[4] Jesus was his chosen lamb. The creator of the universe could have chosen any other day, but he chose *this* Passover at *this* time in history. Why? It goes back to John introducing us to Jesus first and foremost as the "Lamb of God who takes away the sins of the world" (John 1:29).

On the tenth day of the Hebrew month Nisan (their first month according to the Torah), each family selected a clean lamb without defect.[5] The year Jesus was crucified, only lambs born in Bethlehem were considered worthy to be Passover lambs. Although Jesus lived in Nazareth, he was born in Bethlehem because of the census.[6] The

---

4. "When Jesus had finished saying all these things, he said to his disciples, 'As you know, Passover begins in two days, and the Son of Man will be handed over to be crucified.' At that same time the leading priests and elders were meeting at the residence of Caiaphas, the high priest, plotting how to capture Jesus secretly and kill him. 'But not during the Passover celebration,' they agreed, 'or the people may riot'" (Matthew 26:1–4).
5. "While the Israelites were still in the land of Egypt, the Lord gave the following instructions to Moses and Aaron: 'From now on, this month will be the first month of the year for you. Announce to the whole community of Israel that on the tenth day of this month each family must choose a lamb or a young goat for a sacrifice, one animal for each household'" (Exodus 12:1–3).
6. "After Jesus was born in Bethlehem in Judea, during the time of King Herod, Magi from the east came to Jerusalem and asked, 'Where is the one who has been born king of the Jews? We saw his star when it rose and have come to worship him'" (Matthew 2:1–2

priests marched the lambs down the Mount of Olives and entered Jerusalem through the Sheep Gate. Jesus came through the Sheep Gate five days before Passover (on the tenth day of the first month) riding on a donkey.[7] Many Christians know this as the triumphal entry or Palm Sunday. The Father chose Jesus, born in Bethlehem to the virgin Mary, as the people's Passover Lamb. Both Jesus and the lambs, born in Bethlehem, entered through the Sheep Gate on the same day.

It gets even better!

After the chosen lambs entered the Sheep Gate, they were thoroughly inspected by the priests for spots or defects.[8] This week religious leaders investigated Jesus in tandem.[9] He even stood trial before Caiaphas, the high

---

NIV).
7. "Six days before the Passover celebration began, Jesus arrived in Bethany, the home of Lazarus—the man he had raised from the dead. ... The next day, the news that Jesus was on the way to Jerusalem swept through the city. A large crowd of Passover visitors took palm branches and went down the road to meet him. They shouted, 'Praise God! Blessings on the one who comes in the name of the Lord! Hail to the King of Israel!'" (John 12:1, 12–13).
8. "Your lamb shall be without blemish, a male of the first year. You may take it from the sheep or from the goats" (Exodus 12:5 NKJV).
9. "Inside, the high priest began asking Jesus about his followers and what he had been teaching them. Jesus replied, 'Everyone

priest, and Pontius Pilate, the Roman governor.[10] Neither Caiaphas nor Pilate was able to find any fault or blemish in Jesus.[11] A perfect Lamb ready for sacrifice.

Leading up to Passover, Jewish families spent many days removing yeast and any other type of leaven from their homes.[12] Occasionally in Scripture, leavening agents symbolize sin. In 1 Corinthians 5:6–8 Paul wrote, "Your

---

knows what I teach. I have preached regularly in the synagogues and the Temple, where the people gather. I have not spoken in secret. Why are you asking me this question? Ask those who heard me. They know what I said.' Then one of the Temple guards standing nearby slapped Jesus across the face. 'Is that the way to answer the high priest?' he demanded. Jesus replied, 'If I said anything wrong, you must prove it. But if I'm speaking the truth, why are you beating me?' Then Annas bound Jesus and sent him to Caiaphas, the high priest." (John 18:19–24).
10. "Jesus' trial before Caiaphas ended in the early hours of the morning. Then he was taken to the headquarters of the Roman governor. His accusers didn't go inside because it would defile them, and they wouldn't be allowed to celebrate the Passover" (John 18:28).
11. "Pilate went outside again and said to the people, 'I am going to bring him out to you now, but understand clearly that I find him not guilty'" (John 19:4).
12. "Celebrate this Festival of Unleavened Bread, for it will remind you that I brought your forces out of the land of Egypt on this very day. This festival will be a permanent law for you; celebrate this day from generation to generation. ... During those seven days, there must be no trace of yeast in your homes. Anyone who eats anything made with yeast during this week will be cut off from the community of Israel. These regulations apply both to the foreigners living among you and to the native-born Israelites" (Exodus 12:17, 19).

boasting about this is terrible. Don't you realize that this sin is like a little yeast that spreads through the whole batch of dough? Get rid of the old 'yeast' by removing this wicked person from among you. Then you will be like a fresh batch of dough made without yeast, which is what you really are. Christ, our Passover Lamb, has been sacrificed for us. So let us celebrate the festival, not with the old bread of wickedness and evil, but with the new bread of sincerity and truth." Now that all sacrifices have been fulfilled for all eternity by Jesus dying on the cross, we search out "yeast" in our hearts.

Matthew 21:12–13 and Mark 11:15–17 give witness to the final cleansing of God's house, the temple in Jerusalem.[13] Immediately following his entry through the Sheep Gate, Jesus entered the temple. He drove out the people selling animals for sacrifice as well as the money changers. The temple was a den of thieves where merchants robbed and exploited God's children. Jesus cleaned the physical house of God (including under the

---

13. The gospels share many of the same stories and eyewitness accounts of the life of Jesus from four different perspectives. This cleansing of the temple is one event with written witness by two different people.

tables) and then proceeded to clean the people inside God's house through healing and deliverance. The religious leaders heard the people calling Jesus the Son of David and praising him for performing miracles. They began questioning his authority and inspecting our Passover Lamb.

Following thorough examination by the priests, the Passover lambs were led to the altar early in the morning on the fourteenth day of Nisan. They were displayed until the time of sacrifice. Jesus finished the trial with Caiaphas in the early hours of the morning and was taken to Pilate. He was presented to the people (*displayed* if you will) in the purple robe of kings and a crown of thorns. With the deafening shouts of *"Crucify him,"* the people again chose Jesus for their Passover sacrifice.

He trudged to Calvary under the weight of his cross. The Roman soldiers strapped his arms down and nailed his hands and feet to the cross at nine o'clock in the morning[14]—

---

14. Charles Ellicott, *Ellicott's Commentary for English Readers*, Matthew 27:45,
https://biblehub.com/commentaries/ellicott/matthew/27.htm.

the exact time the Passover lambs were strapped to the altar in the temple. Jesus hung there until three o'clock in the afternoon, the time of the evening sacrifice of the Passover lambs. The high priest ascended the altar, cut the lambs' throats to drain their blood, and declared in a loud voice, "*Tetelestai!*" or "It is finished!" The Greek word literally means "the debt is paid in full."[15] At that moment, Jesus gave up his spirit and cried, "*Tetelestai*," and the Lamb of God who came to take away the sins of the world *did just that*.

On the day Jesus died, the Jews prepared for their Sabbath Passover. The religious leaders wanted the three men dead before sundown, the start of a new Hebrew day. Priests weren't allowed to go near or touch dead bodies. If they did, even by accident, they would be cut off from the community for seven days. Passover is an appointed time when God meets with his people. To be cut off from the assembly meant they would not have been able to commune with God during this special time.[16]

---

15. Chuck D. Pierce and Robert Heidler, "Why Passover?" http://www.elijahlist.com/words/display_word/8617.
16. "The high priest has the highest rank of all the priests. The anointing oil has been poured on his head, and he has been ordained to wear the priestly garments. He must never leave his hair

So the leaders requested the legs of the men be broken to speed up the process. The guards broke the shins of the two criminals. However, Jesus was dead when they approached him, making it unnecessary to break his legs.[17]

Back in Exodus 12, after the lambs were slaughtered, God's people roasted the remaining meat. They were commanded to keep it inside their homes and not break any bones.[18] Nearly three thousand years later Jesus, the Passover Lamb, would have no bones broken. The final

---

uncombed or tear his clothing. He must not defile himself by going near a dead body. He may not make himself ceremonially unclean even for his father or mother. He must not defile the sanctuary of his God by leaving it to attend to a dead person, for he has been made holy by the anointing oil of his God. I am the Lord" (Leviticus 21:10–12).

17. "It was the day of preparation, and the Jewish leaders didn't want the bodies hanging there the next day, which was the Sabbath (and a very special Sabbath, because it was Passover week). So they asked Pilate to hasten their deaths by ordering that their legs be broken. Then their bodies could be taken down. So the soldiers came and broke the legs of the two men crucified with Jesus. But when they came to Jesus, they saw that he was already dead, so they didn't break his legs. One of the soldiers, however, pierced his side with a spear, and immediately blood and water flowed out. (This report is from an eyewitness giving an accurate account. He speaks the truth so that you also may continue to believe.) These things happened in fulfillment of the Scriptures that say, 'Not one of his bones will be broken,' and 'They will look on the one they pierced'" (John 19:31–37).

18. "Each Passover lamb must be eaten in one house. Do not carry any of its meat outside, and do not break any of its bones" (Exodus 12:46).

Passover Lamb was sacrificed for all sins past, present, and future just as God originally commanded the fathers to slaughter the Passover lambs in Egypt. Many details run parallel in the accounts of the Passover lambs from Exodus 12 and Jesus's death. God orchestrated countless people and events during this time to fulfill Scripture written thousands of years earlier.

If you weren't convinced that God is in the details, I truly hope this helps. Every little detail is important, planned, and expertly executed. On top of that, everyone still had their own choices. Peter was warned about his denial of Christ, Judas was exposed at the table before his betrayal, yet God's purpose prevailed. My reason for deeply exploring Passover is to help you get to know Jesus and how the details make all the difference. As I continue to study Scripture, I notice God's attention to detail with everything that he says and does. His words are intentional. He uses them to create galaxies. Every star has a name.[19] *This is* the God we serve. I stopped believing in coincidence a long time ago. He's just too

---

19. "He counts the stars and calls them all by name. How great is our Lord! His power is absolute! His understanding is beyond comprehension!" (Psalm 147:4–5)

big and too powerful and too creative to let something like "chance" happen.

Bear with me for just a moment more as we continue this study of the Passover Lamb, Jesus.[20] One Scripture study technique I like to employ is the "law of first mention."[21] It answers the question, "Where is the word '*kiḇ·śōṯ*,' or lamb, first mentioned in the Bible?" This helps us see the original intent and context. The first mention is Genesis 21:28, which states, "Abraham set apart seven ewe lambs from the flock" (NIV). Abraham and Abimelech made a treaty to live peacefully together in the land. One of Abimelech's servants seized a well Abraham dug, which was a clear violation of the peace treaty. Abraham brought this to Abimelech's attention. They made another agreement, and Abraham set apart the seven ewe (female) lambs as a witness that he actually dug the well in question. Abimelech accepted the lambs, and they

---

20. "Get rid of the old 'yeast' by removing this wicked person from among you. Then you will be like a fresh batch of dough made without yeast, which is what you really are. Christ, our Passover Lamb, has been sacrificed for us" (1 Corinthians 5:7).
21. Got Questions, "What is the law of first mention?" https://www.gotquestions.org/law-of-first-mention.html.

swore an oath. The lambs were a sign to Abimelech that Abraham was telling the truth.

In Revelation 1, John wrote messages from Jesus to the seven churches. In this final book of the Bible, God revealed Jesus in his glorious form to John. Just as Abraham brought lambs as a witness to the truth, John began his letter to the churches describing Jesus as "the faithful witness, firstborn from the dead, and the ruler of the kings of the earth."[22] From the beginning of time and Scripture (Genesis) to the end (Revelation), Jesus is *the* witness to the truth. "Jesus answered, 'I am the way and the truth and the life. No one comes to the Father except through me'" (John 14:6). *Jesus is the truth!* There is no other way to God except through Jesus. Just as the details of Jesus's life are intricately woven, so are yours. He made careful plans for each moment of your life. My prayer for you today is that you would begin to see how God put together details in your life—how he has his hand in every little moment!

---

22. "Grace and peace to you from him who is, and who was, and who is to come, and from the seven spirits before his throne, and from Jesus Christ, who is the faithful witness, the firstborn from the dead, and the ruler of the kings of the earth" (Revelation 1:4–5 NIV).

Thank you, God, for the details of our lives. "You made all the delicate, inner parts of my body and knit me together in my mother's womb. Thank you for making me so wonderfully complex! Your workmanship is marvelous—how well I know it. You watched me as I was being formed in utter seclusion, as I was woven together in the dark of the womb. You saw me before I was born. Every day of my life was recorded in your book. Every moment was laid out before a single day had passed. How precious are your thoughts about me, O God. They cannot be numbered! I can't even count them; they outnumber the grains of sand! And when I wake up, you are still with me!" (Psalm 139:13–18). How you painstakingly counted every hair and every cell in every person. Would you show us how much care you took with every detail of our lives? God, you are so

> good. You even take things that we mess up or that the enemy uses to harm us and turn them around for our good![23] Nothing is wasted with you—no experience, no tear, no pain, no suffering. You said you will turn it all for our benefit! And we say thank you!

Beloved, if you ever doubt God called you, trust his Word. "God is faithful, who has called you into fellowship with his Son, Jesus Christ our Lord" (1 Corinthians 1:9 NIV). If you have accepted Jesus and all he has done for you through death and resurrection, you have been called! I also want to assure you that God calls to everyone, but some do not answer on this side of eternity. "The Lord isn't really being slow about his promise, as some people think. No, he is being patient for your sake. He does not want anyone to be destroyed but wants everyone to repent. But the day of the Lord will come as unexpectedly as a thief. Then the heavens will pass away with a terrible noise, and the very

---

23. "And we know that God causes everything to work together for the good of those who love God and are called according to his purpose for them" (Romans 8:28).

elements themselves will disappear in fire, and the earth and everything on it will be found to deserve judgment" (2 Peter 3:9–10). As long as people are alive, there's hope they will hear God's call and invite him in. If we're truly disciples of Jesus, even death doesn't have a final say when the same Spirit that raised Jesus from the dead lives inside of us!

CHAPTER 3

"He Existed Long Before Me"

"The next day John saw Jesus coming toward him and said, 'Look! The Lamb of God who takes away the sin of the world! He is the one I was talking about when I said, "A man is coming after me who is far greater than I am, for he existed long before me." I did not recognize him as the Messiah, but I have been baptizing with water so that he might be revealed to Israel'" (John 1:29–31).

In the Scripture referenced above, God speaks to John about Jesus and the Holy Spirit. We've discovered Jesus as the Lamb of God and how he took away the sins of the world. Next, we're going to explore John's statement, "he existed long before me." Mary, the mother of Jesus, and her relative Elizabeth, the mother of John, were pregnant at the same time.[1] John was roughly six months older than Jesus. So how did Jesus exist long before John?

"In the beginning the Word already existed. The Word was with God, and the Word was God. He existed in the beginning with God" (John 1:1–2). Jesus is the "the Word" referenced in this Scripture. If it were simply understood that Jesus was with God in the beginning, why would Holy Spirit inspire John to write these words?[2] Why would it be necessary to point out that Jesus existed with God in the beginning? Perhaps to show they had a discussion as Holy Spirit hovered over the deep waters they were about to fill. On the day God

---

1. "The angel replied, 'The Holy Spirit will come upon you, and the power of the Most High will overshadow you. So the baby to be born will be holy, and he will be called the Son of God. What's more, your relative Elizabeth has become pregnant in her old age! People used to say she was barren, but she has conceived a son and is now in her sixth month. For the word of God will never fail'" (Luke 1:35–37).
2. "And so we have the prophetic word confirmed, which you do well to heed as a light that shines in a dark place, until the day dawns and the morning star rises in your hearts; knowing this first, that no prophecy of Scripture is of any private interpretation, for prophecy never came by the will of man, but holy men of God spoke as they were moved by the Holy Spirit" (2 Peter 1:19–21 NKJV).

created man, "God said, 'Let us make human beings in our image, to be like us. They will reign over the fish in the sea, the birds in the sky, the livestock, all the wild animals on the earth, and the small animals that scurry along the ground'" (Genesis 1:26). The name for God throughout Genesis 1 is *Elohim*, which is plural.[3] I believe God had a conversation with Jesus about what man and woman should look like. The shift in wording in verse 26 gives a glimpse into that conversation between the two.

Up to this point in Scripture, it might sound like God created the heavens, planets, animals, and everything else without discussing it with Jesus. We know that isn't true because John 1:3 states, "God created everything through him, and nothing was created except through him [Jesus]." The Christian Standard Bible says, "all things were created." When God says all, he means *all*. Nothing is excluded, and I believe that is why he says the same thing two different ways. It's important because God is consistent.[4]

---

3. James Strong, *Strong's Lexicon*, Genesis 1:1, https://biblehub.com/parallel/genesis/1-1.htm.
4. "Jesus Christ is the same yesterday, today, and forever" (Hebrews

Did you know that Jesus was the firstborn of all creation? "Christ is the visible image of the invisible God. He existed before anything was created and is supreme over all creation, for through him God created everything in the heavenly realms and on earth. He made the things we can see and the things we can't see—such as thrones, kingdoms, rulers, and authorities in the unseen world. Everything was created through him and for him. He existed before anything else, and he holds all creation together" (Colossians 1:15–17). Not only did he exist long ago, but he holds all creation together even now. *Wow!*

So that is great news about Jesus; but what about us? Where were we at the beginning of time? Did God plan out every moment of our lives as intricately as he did for Jesus? You might be thinking that your story starts the day you were conceived, but God says differently.

> You made all the delicate, inner parts of
> my body and knit me together in my

13:8).

mother's womb. Thank you for making me so wonderfully complex! Your workmanship is marvelous—how well I know it. You watched me as I was being formed in utter seclusion, as I was woven together in the dark of the womb. You saw me before I was born. Every day of my life was recorded in your book. Every moment was laid out before a single day had passed. How precious are your thoughts about me, O God. They cannot be numbered! I can't even count them; they outnumber the grains of sand! And when I wake up, you are still with me! (Psalm 139:13–18)

You and I were so important to God that he planned our days before anything else was created. It blows my mind. He knew the plans of the enemy for our lives, our own will and sin, and every other factor surrounding us in this world. He chose to create all of us knowing it would cost him his very life. He is in every detail. He wasn't about to leave us to chance. God had an original plan and purpose for you before sin ever entered the world, and he is not thrown off one bit by our sin or the enemy. He is so big and so powerful that he can still accomplish his original plan for each of us in this crazy world. God is so incredibly detail oriented.

God, thank you for creating the people reading this book. I pray as they read about who you are and what you have done for them that you would wrap your giant daddy arms around them. Let them rest in you. Help them relax in your embrace and trust you because you are big! You care about every single detail ... good, bad, and indifferent. You have called every single one of them and you have always had a plan! Reveal yourself to them in ways they have never experienced before. Help them to see and hear and know you are the one true God. Thank you for each person reading this prayer. I am excited to hear the testimonies and stories of how you are speaking to them! Bless them with understanding and insight! Help them to know you more. In Jesus's name.

CHAPTER 4

Baptism

John met Jesus for the first time when they were both in the womb.[1] John had a special assignment and call from God. The angel Gabriel told John's father, Zechariah, that his wife would have a son. They were to name him John and he needed to stay away from alcohol.[2]

---

1. "When Elizabeth heard Mary's greeting, the baby leaped in her womb, and Elizabeth was filled with the Holy Spirit. In a loud voice she exclaimed: 'Blessed are you among women, and blessed is the child you will bear! But why am I so favored, that the mother of my Lord should come to me? As soon as the sound of your greeting reached my ears, the baby in my womb leaped for joy. Blessed is she who has believed that the Lord would fulfill his promises to her!" (Luke 1:41–45).
2. "While Zechariah was in the sanctuary, an angel of the Lord appeared to him, standing to the right of the incense altar. Zechariah was shaken and overwhelmed with fear when he saw him. But the angel said, 'Don't be afraid, Zechariah! God has heard your prayer. Your wife, Elizabeth, will give you a son, and you are to name him John. You will have great joy and gladness, and many will rejoice at

I can only imagine how drinking excessively and acting foolish one time would have completely discredited John's ministry. His testimony of Jesus would be tarnished. John wore clothes made of animal skin and ate locusts and honey.[3] This was a nice way of saying he was a little strange. He was bold and wild, even without alcohol. Scripture also says John was filled with the Holy Spirit from the time he was conceived. I believe this is why he moved in Elizabeth's belly when he heard Mary speaking.[4] The Spirit within him leapt at the Spirit within Mary. John prepared the way for the Messiah.[5] Since both John's mother and father were from a lineage of priests, John was a priest also.[6]

---

his birth, for he will be great in the eyes of the Lord. He must never touch wine or other alcoholic drinks. He will be filled with the Holy Spirit, even before his birth'" (Luke 1:11).
3. "John's clothes were woven from coarse camel hair, and he wore a leather belt around his waist. For food he ate locusts and wild honey" (Matthew 3:4).
4. "A few days later Mary hurried to the hill country of Judea, to the town where Zechariah lived. She entered the house and greeted Elizabeth. At the sound of Mary's greeting, Elizabeth's child leaped within her, and Elizabeth was filled with the Holy Spirit" (Luke 1:39–41).
5. "The prophet Isaiah was speaking about John when he said, 'He is a voice shouting in the wilderness, "Prepare the way for the Lord's coming! Clear the road for him!"'" (Matthew 3:3).
6. "When Herod was king of Judea, there was a Jewish priest named Zechariah. He was a member of the priestly order of Abijah, and his wife, Elizabeth, was also from the priestly line of Aaron" (Luke

Now that we know a little more about John, let's explore this last portion of his testimony about Jesus. "I did not recognize him as the Messiah, but I have been baptizing with water so that he might be revealed to Israel" (John 1:31). God wanted his people, the Hebrews, to recognize Jesus as the Messiah first.

How did John know to baptize with water? *God told him!* He sent John to baptize with water. God gave him specific details about what to watch for when he baptized people. "Then John testified, 'I saw the Holy Spirit descending like a dove from heaven and resting upon him. I didn't know he was the one, but when God sent me to baptize with water, he told me, "The one on whom you see the Spirit descend and rest is the one who will baptize with the Holy Spirit." I saw this happen to Jesus, so I testify that he is the Chosen One of God'" (John 1:32–34). Not only did God send John as a witness to reveal Jesus as the Messiah, the Father spoke from heaven and confirmed that Jesus is his Son.[7]

1:5).
7. "One day when the crowds were being baptized, Jesus himself was baptized. As he was praying, the heavens opened, and the Holy

When Jesus rose from the water, John saw the Holy Spirit descend on him and remain. The Greek word translated "remain" is *menō*. It means "to remain or abide, equivalent to not to depart, not to leave, to continue to be present: to put forth constant influence upon one, of the Holy Spirit."[8] The Holy Spirit came on Jesus and *never* left. He took up residence and refused to move out!

In this one baptism, Jesus was revealed to Israel, the Holy Spirit came upon him, and his true identity as the Son of God was revealed. In these passages we are studying, it may sound like there are two different baptisms—one with water and one with the Holy Spirit (fire)—but Ephesians 4 6 says there is one baptism.[9] I wrestled with this when I was young because Scripture

---

Spirit, in bodily form, descended on him like a dove. And a voice from heaven said, 'You are my dearly loved Son, and you bring me great joy'" (Luke 3:21–22).
8. James Strong, *Strong's Lexicon*, John 1:33, https://biblehub.com/greek/3306.htm
9. "There is one body and one Spirit, just as you were called to one hope when you were called; one Lord, one faith, one baptism; one God and Father of all, who is over all and through all and in all" Ephesians 4:4–6.

does not lie or contradict itself. There must be something I was missing. What I was taught and heard from my leadership didn't line up with what I read and understood from God's Word.

This is where the Holy Spirit steps in and brings understanding. "But when the Father sends the Advocate as my representative—that is, the Holy Spirit—he will teach you everything and will remind you of everything I have told you" (John 14:26). If we step back for help and understanding, he is faithful to do it. God is not trying to hide himself from us or make things cryptic. "But it was to us that God revealed these things by his Spirit. For his Spirit searches out everything and shows us God's deep secrets. No one can know a person's thoughts except that person's own spirit, and no one can know God's thoughts except God's own Spirit. And we have received God's Spirit (not the world's spirit), so we can know the wonderful things God has freely given us" (1 Corinthians 2:10–12).

Some teach there is only water baptism and others only fire baptism. Just like Father, Son, and Holy Spirit are three in one, baptism is comprised of multiple parts in one.

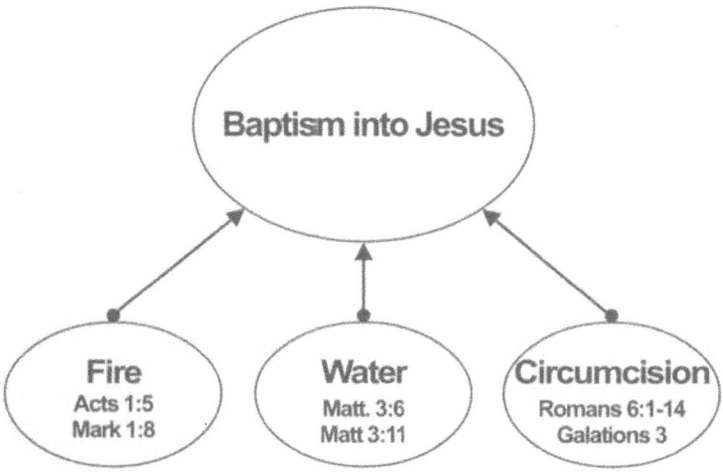

In our lives, we may experience all of these events at different times. For instance, I was baptized with water at age nine, baptized with the Holy Spirit at age eleven, and regularly undergo spiritual circumcision as Jesus reveals areas needing to be cut off.[10] My husband has a similar timeline between water and fire baptism. Does that mean we experienced two different baptisms? *No!*

---

10. "When you came to Christ, you were 'circumcised,' but not by a physical procedure. Christ performed a spiritual circumcision—the cutting away of your sinful nature. For you were buried with Christ when you were baptized. And with him you were raised to new life because you trusted the mighty power of God, who raised Christ from the dead" (Colossians 2:11–12).

God is outside of time. He is not bound by our timelines.[11] The psalmist reveals, "A thousand years in your sight are like a day that has just gone by, or like a watch in the night" (Psalm 90:4 NIV). No matter when these events happen in our walk with God, it will only ever be a single day on his calendar. The important key is that all these events *must* happen.

Don't take my word for it. Go to Acts 19. Paul traveled to the village of Ephesus. His first encounter with disciples of Jesus is documented in verse 2. Paul asks, "Did you receive the Holy Spirit *when you believed*?"[12] There is further discussion in that chapter about which baptism these people received. Accounting for two separate baptisms: one from John and the other from Jesus. John's baptism was designed to prepare the hearts for Jesus and his baptism. John's baptism did not provide salvation, deliverance, or the Holy Spirit. It was only for repentance of sins. Baptism into Jesus now encompasses John's baptism of repentance.

---

11. "But do not forget this one thing, dear friends: With the Lord, a day is like a thousand years, and a thousand years are like a day" (2 Peter 3:8).
12. Emphasis added.

CHAPTER 5

"The Spirit Will Tell You"

"When the Spirit of truth comes, he will guide you into all truth. He will not speak on his own but will tell you what he has heard. He will tell you about the future. He will bring me glory by telling you whatever he receives from me. All that belongs to the Father is mine; this is why I said, 'The Spirit will tell you whatever he receives from me'" (John 16:13–15). Jesus is speaking to his disciples.

This Scripture reaffirms how God the Father, Jesus his Son, and the Holy Spirit are all connected and one. So why was it important for Jesus to specify who would speak to the disciples? Why would that matter? Words are important to God. I do not believe for one minute the Creator of the universe and all that is in it flippantly decided who would speak and when in his epic narrative, the Bible. God spoke and planets formed out of *nothing*.[1] God's words are uttered intentionally and with purpose.

As we discussed earlier, we serve one God in three persons. Each person of the Godhead has a different relationship dynamic. While walking the earth, Jesus said God is Father.[2] The Father called Jesus his Son after his baptism and throughout Scripture.[3] This same concept is at work in our lives. I am a wife, a mother, and a daughter. In each of these relationships, I am called different names like Sweetie, Mom, and Tiss based on how the person talking to me relates. Please understand that these attributes of the Father, the Son,

---

1. "By faith we understand that the entire universe was formed at God's command, that what we now see did not come from anything that can be seen" (Hebrews 1:3).
2. "Jesus replied, 'If I glorify myself, my glory means nothing. My Father, whom you claim as your God, is the one who glorifies me'" (John 8:54 NIV).
3. "Then a cloud overshadowed them, and a voice from the cloud said, 'This is my dearly loved Son. Listen to him'" (Mark 9:7); "For to which of the angels did God ever say, 'You are my Son; today I have become your Father' Or again, 'I will be his Father, and he will be my Son'?" (Hebrews 1:5 NIV).

and the Holy Spirit do not restrict them. They are not confined by any of their names. In fact, they help *us* to relate to and understand God's character more deeply. They are for our benefit.

Each time the Israelites gave God a new description or name in the Bible, it was because they understood their relationship with him in a different way. Yeshua (Jesus) is God's name that helps us relate to him in human flesh.[4] The name "Jesus" is God's name for his human body, and it is the name that protects and unifies those who are his. Jesus left the earth so God could send the Holy Spirit to us.[5] He is purposeful with his words. The Holy Spirit is the dynamic of God residing in Heaven and on the

---

4. [Jesus said,] "I will remain in the world no longer, but they are still in the world, and I am coming to you. Holy Father, protect them by the power of your name, the name you gave me, so that they may be one as we are one. While I was with them, I protected them and kept them safe by that name you gave me. None has been lost except the one doomed to destruction so that Scripture would be fulfilled" (John 17:11–12 NIV).
5. "But very truly I tell you, it is for your good that I am going away. Unless I go away, the Advocate will not come to you; but if I go, I will send him to you. When he comes, he will prove the world to be in the wrong about sin and righteousness and judgment: about sin, because people do not believe in me; about righteousness, because I am going to the Father, where you can see me no longer; and about judgment, because the prince of this world now stands condemned" (John 16:7–11 NIV).

earth. "For there are three that bear witness in heaven: the Father, the Word, and the Holy Spirit; and these three are one. And there are three that bear witness on earth: the Spirit, the water, and the blood; and these three agree as one" (1 John 5:7–8 NKJV). He is the one we interact with the most and understanding his character and name helps us build relationship.

Before Jesus ascended into Heaven, he spoke of the Holy Spirit who would come and dwell within us[6] and upon us.[7] Jesus instructed the disciples to wait until this gift came to them.[8] They remained in that room for ten days.[9]

---

6. "The Spirit of God, who raised Jesus from the dead, lives in you. And just as God raised Christ Jesus from the dead, he will give life to your mortal bodies by this same Spirit living within you" (Romans 8:11).
7. "But you will receive power when the Holy Spirit comes upon you. And you will be my witnesses, telling people about me everywhere—in Jerusalem, throughout Judea, in Samaria, and to the ends of the earth" (Acts 1:8).
8. "Once when he was eating with them, he commanded them, 'Do not leave Jerusalem until the Father sends you the gift he promised, as I told you before. John baptized with water, but in just a few days you will be baptized with the Holy Spirit'" (Acts 1:4–5).
9. "On the day of Pentecost all the believers were meeting together in one place. Suddenly, there was a sound from heaven like the roaring of a mighty windstorm, and it filled the house where they were sitting. Then, what looked like flames or tongues of fire appeared and settled on each of them. And everyone present was filled with the Holy Spirit and began speaking in other languages, as the Holy Spirit gave them this ability" (Acts 2:1–4).

Can you imagine waiting somewhere with no less than 120 people for *ten days*? Without a cell phone or television? How about waiting and not really knowing what to expect? Or how the gift will be delivered? Were they startled each time someone knocked at the door? Do you wonder about these things too?

Isn't it easier to wait patiently for friends to arrive? You anticipate their arrival and endure the wait if they tarry. This could by a reason Jesus spoke so often of Holy Spirit as our friend, our comforter, and our companion.[10] Perhaps to encourage the disciples in their waiting. In the end, 120 people followed the command to wait. It could be these believers understood what to expect when the Holy Spirit arrived. Those who remained certainly trusted Jesus and obeyed to the end ... or should I say the beginning! This incredible gift of the Holy Spirit is a trustworthy friend who is like no other and certainly worth the wait.

A time will come in your journey where you will have to trust you are hearing God. Becoming familiar with the

---

10. See John 14–16.

Bible is crucial for telling the difference between your own thoughts and the Holy Spirit's voice.[11] Recall the voice of a close friend or relative you love and talk to often. Would you quickly recognize their voice over the phone or with your eyes closed? You might know the person so well you can even identify them when their voice is distorted because of a cold or bad phone signal. The same is true of the Holy Spirit. He speaks from within us because our body is his temple or home.[12] He lives inside us and we carry his presence everywhere we go. The Holy Spirit is within us as a seal or stamp showing we belong to God.[13]

---

11. "The Spirit searches all things, even the deep things of God. For who knows a person's thoughts except their own spirit within them? In the same way no one knows the thoughts of God except the Spirit of God. What we have received is not the spirit of the world, but the Spirit who is from God, so that we may understand what God has freely given us" (1 Corinthians 2:10–12 NIV).
12. "Don't you realize that your body is the temple of the Holy Spirit, who lives in you and was given to you by God? You do not belong to yourself, for God bought you with a high price. So you must honor God with your body" (1 Corinthians 6:19–20).
13. "And you also were included in Christ when you heard the message of truth, the gospel of your salvation. When you believed, you were marked in him with a seal, the promised Holy Spirit, who is a deposit guaranteeing our inheritance until the redemption of those who are God's possession—to the praise of his glory" (Ephesians 1:13–14 NIV).

Immersing us in fire, the Holy Spirit purifies and empowers us to do God's will.[14] Remember, the Spirit only tells us what he hears from Jesus, and Jesus only says what he hears from the Father.[15] We want to be like Jesus in this way. Our desire when we speak and act should be to do what we hear the Father doing and say what we hear the Father saying.[16]

> Anyone who isn't with me opposes me, and anyone who isn't working with me is actually working against me.

> So I tell you, every sin and blasphemy can be forgiven—except blasphemy against the Holy Spirit, which will never be forgiven. Anyone who speaks against the Son of Man can be forgiven, but anyone who speaks against the Holy Spirit will

---

14. See Acts 1–2.
15. "All that belongs to the Father is mine; this is why I said, 'The Spirit will tell you whatever he receives from me'" (John 16:15).
16. "So Jesus explained, 'I tell you the truth, the Son can do nothing by himself. He does only what he sees the Father doing. Whatever the Father does, the Son also does'" (John 5:19).

never be forgiven, either in this world or in the world to come.

A tree is identified by its fruit. If a tree is good, its fruit will be good. If a tree is bad, its fruit will be bad. You brood of snakes! How could evil men like you speak what is good and right? For whatever is in your heart determines what you say. A good person produces good things from the treasury of a good heart, and an evil person produces evil things from the treasury of an evil heart. And I tell you this, you must give an account on judgment day for every idle word you speak. The words you say will either acquit you or condemn you. (Matthew 12:30–37)

Why did Jesus say that our idle words will either acquit or condemn us? From Scripture, we know there is no condemnation for those who belong to Jesus. "So now there is no condemnation for those who belong to Christ

Jesus. And because you belong to him, the power of the life-giving Spirit has freed you from the power of sin that leads to death" (Romans 8:1–2). Jesus was not contradicting himself. Whether we realize it or not, we are continuously accused by Satan in the Courtroom of Heaven.[17] Our sin builds his case against us. God is a just Judge and runs his court similar to our court proceedings. We need to show up in court through prayer to plead the blood of Jesus over our sin and ask forgiveness. There is life and death in the tongue. Our words are binding agreements that give the enemy rights to areas of our life while on Earth. When we speak evil, we fuel the enemy's testimony against us. These idle words will determine whether we live the abundant life God meant for us on this side of eternity or if we will

---

17. "Then I heard a loud voice shouting across the heavens, 'It has come at last— salvation and power and the Kingdom of our God, and the authority of his Christ. For the accuser of our brothers and sisters has been thrown down to earth— the one who accuses them before our God day and night. And they have defeated him by the blood of the Lamb and by their testimony. And they did not love their lives so much that they were afraid to die. Therefore, rejoice, O heavens! And you who live in the heavens, rejoice! But terror will come on the earth and the sea, for the devil has come down to you in great anger, knowing that he has little time.' And the dragon was angry at the woman and declared war against the rest of her children—all who keep God's commandments and maintain their testimony for Jesus" (Revelation 12:10-12,17).

live condemned and bound by the enemy. We can ask God to nullify or rescind every idle word we've spoken because of the blood of Jesus. For more information and resources about the courtroom of Heaven and living an abundant life, see the appendices.

CHAPTER 6

Why Is the Holy Spirit Important?

The Holy Spirit has been influencing your life and directing your path from the beginning. The reason we believe Jesus is the Son of God is because the Holy Spirit revealed him to us. "The person without the Spirit does not accept the things that come from the Spirit of God but considers them foolishness and cannot understand them because they are discerned only through the Spirit. The person with the Spirit makes judgments about all things, but such a person is not subject to merely human judgments, for, 'Who has known the mind of the Lord so as to instruct him?' But we have the mind of Christ" (1 Corinthians 2:14–16 NIV). I want to give you practical ways to build an intimate relationship with the Holy Spirit so you can live by the Spirit.[1] In the previous chapter, we spent time discovering *who* the Holy Spirit is. Now we'll explore why he is important in this new covenant time after Jesus.[2]

It is the Holy Spirit *through* Jesus that gives us the confidence we belong to God. It is important that you receive the Holy Spirit through Jesus. "Peter replied, 'Each of you must repent of your sins and turn to God and be baptized in the name of Jesus Christ for the forgiveness of your sins. Then you will receive the gift of the Holy Spirit" (Acts 2:38).

Any spirit received outside of surrender to Jesus is not the Holy Spirit. "Not everyone who calls out to me, 'Lord! Lord!' will enter the Kingdom of Heaven. Only those who actually do the will of my Father in heaven will enter. On judgment day many will say to me, 'Lord!

---

1. "Since we are living by the Spirit, let us follow the Spirit's leading in every part of our lives" (Galatians 5:25).
2. "He has enabled us to be ministers of his new covenant. This is a covenant not of written laws, but of the Spirit. The old written covenant ends in death; but under the new covenant, the Spirit gives life" (2 Corinthians 3:6).

Lord! We prophesied in your name and cast out demons in your name and performed many miracles in your name.' But I will reply, 'I never knew you. Get away from me, you who break God's laws'" (Matthew 7:21–23). From John 16:15, we know that we cannot do the will of God *without* the Holy Spirit.[3]

Fan into Flame

In 2 Timothy 1:6–7, Paul reminded Timothy to fan into flame the gift of God. Paul laid hands on Timothy earlier in the text and baptized him with the Holy Spirit.[4] The Greek citizens watched as Paul laid hands on Timothy. They saw the power of God in Paul and Timothy through the visible workings of the Holy Spirit. Remember the Holy Spirit is the gift we are fanning into flame. So how do we do that? We give him what he wants! Praise,

---

3. "All that belongs to the Father is mine; this is why I said, 'The Spirit will tell you whatever he receives from me'" (John 16:15).
4. "This is why I remind you to fan into flames the spiritual gift God gave you when I laid my hands on you. For God has not given us a spirit of fear and timidity, but of power, love, and self–discipline" (2 Timothy 1:6–7); "Do not neglect your gift, which was given you through prophecy when the body of elders laid their hands on you" (1 Timothy 4:14 NIV).

worship, adoration, and attention. "The Lord your God is a devouring fire; he is a jealous God. In the future, when you have children and grandchildren and have lived in the land a long time, do not corrupt yourselves by making idols of any kind. This is evil in the sight of the Lord your God and will arouse his anger" (Deuteronomy 4:24–25). He is jealous for *us*!

Reading the Bible, meditating on Scriptures, singing songs and prayer are great ways to fan the flame of the Holy Spirit inside of you little by little every day. A spark can turn into a blaze with a small, continuous breeze. Pour lighter fluid on a fire for large flashy flame, but it dies as quickly as it started. This is great for starting the fire or quickly fueling it, but it doesn't keep the flame going. Weekend events like church and special conferences are lighter fluid to our spirits. We get a quick boost, but it won't sustain us when we return home. I believe we need both types of fuel for our fire. Can you think of other ways you can fan the flame of the Holy Spirit in your life? Make a commitment and plan to incorporate both "lighter fluid" events as well as daily "continuous breezes" into your week. He is faithful to meet you.[5]

Quenching the Fire

The Holy Spirit can also be quenched or put out like a fire.[6] Sin is like water to his fire. Ephesians 4:17–32 tells us to throw off the old way of living and sinful nature we had before we learned the truth of Jesus. It grieves the Holy Spirit when we are not kind, tender–hearted, and forgiving towards one another.[7] Additionally, if the fire is not fed regularly, it will die out. We are to continually grow up in God and remain in the faith. Paul shares the

---

5. "It was by faith that Enoch was taken up to heaven without dying—'he disappeared, because God took him.' For before he was taken up, he was known as a person who pleased God. And it is impossible to please God without faith. Anyone who wants to come to him must believe that God exists and that he rewards those who sincerely seek him" (Hebrews 11:5–6).
6. "Do not quench the Spirit" (1 Thessalonians 5:19 NIV).
7. "Don't use foul or abusive language. Let everything you say be good and helpful, so that your words will be an encouragement to those who hear them. And do not bring sorrow to God's Holy Spirit by the way you live. Remember, he has identified you as his own, guaranteeing that you will be saved on the day of redemption. Get rid of all bitterness, rage, anger, harsh words, and slander, as well as all types of evil behavior. Instead, be kind to each other, tenderhearted, forgiving one another, just as God through Christ has forgiven you" (Ephesians 4:29-32).

dangers of letting the flame fizzle out in his letter to the believers in Colossae. "But you must continue to believe this truth and stand firmly in it. Don't drift away from the assurance you received when you heard the Good News. The Good News has been preached all over the world, and I, Paul, have been appointed as God's servant to proclaim it" (Colossians 1:23). The Good News is the death and resurrection of Jesus *and* the gift of the Holy Spirit.

Bill Johnson, Senior Leader at Bethel Church, gives a great visual explanation of the Holy Spirit as a dove on our shoulder.[8] Doves are easily startled. If we had one sitting on our shoulder, we'd be mindful of it, gently stepping to keep from disturbing it. Every move we'd make would have the comfort of the bird at the forefront of our mind. What if we lived our lives like this for the Holy Spirit? Every word, every thought, every action weighed against Ephesians 4 as well as the whole of Scripture to determine if it would grieve him.

---

8. Bill Johnson, "Hosting the Presence," YouTube video, 31:32, posted by gatewaychurchtv, November 30, 2016, https://youtu.be/4lL3vVFxG2E.

Throughout God's Word, the Holy Spirit empowered people to do amazing things, like David slaying Goliath.[9] He gave Gideon courage and military strategy to lead the tiny army of three hundred Israelites against 135,000 Midianite soldiers.[10] Remember Samson crushing the Philistines in one blow,[11] and Elijah running faster than Ahab's chariot after killing 850 prophets of Baal?[12] The Holy Spirit transported Philip fifty-seven miles from Samaria to Azotus (present day Ashdod) in the blink of an eye.[13] All of this accomplished by the Spirit of God (through humans), who we have learned is the Holy Spirit.

---

9. "So as David stood there among his brothers, Samuel took the flask of olive oil he had brought and anointed David with the oil. And the Spirit of the Lord came powerfully upon David from that day on. Then Samuel returned to Ramah" (1 Samuel 16:13) and 1 Samuel 17.
10. "But the Spirit of the Lord came upon Gideon" (Judges 6:34 KJV).
11. "As Samson arrived at Lehi, the Philistines came shouting in triumph. But the Spirit of the Lord came powerfully upon Samson, and he snapped the ropes on his arms as if they were burnt strands of flax, and they fell from his wrists. Then he found the jawbone of a recently killed donkey. He picked it up and killed 1,000 Philistines with it" (Judges 15:14–15).
12. 1 Kings 18.
13. "When they came up out of the water, the Spirit of the Lord snatched Philip away. The eunuch never saw him again but went on his way rejoicing. Meanwhile, Philip found himself farther north at the town of Azotus. He preached the Good News there and in every town along the way until he came to Caesarea" (Acts 8:39–40).

When Jesus was baptized, he came up out of the water full of the Holy Spirit.[14] Jesus then followed God's Spirit into the desert to endure temptation from the enemy for forty days. Trials and temptations are the Holy Spirit's invitation into our own desert experience. He wants to purify and sanctify us. We see Jesus's warfare strategy here also. He uses fasting and God's Word against the temptations of the enemy. We're not perfect so it takes a little longer than forty days for us to grasp these lessons.[15] God does not do the tempting,[16] but he allows us to come to that place. Every time you resist the temptations of the enemy and speak God's Word to your situation, you are growing and maturing. See Luke 4 and Matthew 4 to explore this part of Jesus's life in greater detail.

---

14. "Then Jesus, full of the Holy Spirit, returned from the Jordan River. He was led by the Spirit in the wilderness" (Luke 4:1).
15. "May God himself, the God of peace, sanctify you through and through. May your whole spirit, soul and body be kept blameless at the coming of our Lord Jesus Christ. The one who calls you is faithful, and he will do it" (1 Thessalonians 5:23–24 NIV).
16. "And remember, when you are being tempted, do not say, 'God is tempting me.' God is never tempted to do wrong, and he never tempts anyone else" (James 1 13).

After resisting the temptations of Satan, Jesus left the desert full of the power of the Holy Spirit. James, through the Holy Spirit,[17] tells us to consider it all joy when we encounter difficulties or temptations.[18] Who can really do this on their own? I know I can't, not for long anyway, and not with difficult trials. I'm just being honest here. But God commands us to count it all joy, so how do we obey? The Holy Spirit teaches us how to obey these seemingly impossible commands.[19] Surrendering to his leading brings deeper relationship and the power of the Holy Spirit.

God values people more than anything else in his kingdom. He went to great lengths to restore relationship with us.[20] If we seek power without relationship, we

---

17. "All Scripture is inspired by God and is useful to teach us what is true and to make us realize what is wrong in our lives. It corrects us when we are wrong and teaches us to do what is right. God uses it to prepare and equip his people to do every good work" (2 Timothy 3:16–17).
18. "Dear brothers and sisters, when troubles of any kind come your way, consider it an opportunity for great joy. For you know that when your faith is tested, your endurance has a chance to grow" (James 1:2–3).
19. "Jesus looked at them intently and said, 'Humanly speaking, it is impossible. But not with God. Everything is possible with God'" (Mark 10:27).
20. "Then times of refreshment will come from the presence of the Lord, and he will again send you Jesus, your appointed Messiah. For

become like Simon the sorcerer in Acts 8. Through divination and magic, he experienced power and fame outside of God. All Samaria followed him.

Philip shared the gospel in Samaria. Simon believed the good news[21] of salvation through Jesus and was baptized.[22] He followed Philip and witnessed many miracles. Soon Peter and John heard about the explosions of faith in Samaria. They went to lay hands on believers and prayed they would receive the Holy Spirit. Everyone they laid hands on received this wonderful gift. Simon saw the power of the Holy Spirit released through the apostles. He asked them if he could buy the ability to impart power and the Holy Spirit to those he touched. They told him to pray to God and

---

he must remain in heaven until the time for the final restoration of all things, as God promised long ago through his holy prophets" (Acts 3:20–21).
21. "Always remember that Jesus Christ, a descendant of King David, was raised from the dead. This is the Good News I preach" (2 Timothy 2:8).
22. "But now the people believed Philip's message of Good News concerning the Kingdom of God and the name of Jesus Christ. As a result, many men and women were baptized. Then Simon himself believed and was baptized. He began following Philip wherever he went, and he was amazed by the signs and great miracles Philip performed" Acts 8:12).

repent for the bitterness and sin in his heart. Simon asked them to pray to God *for* him.[23]

Simon believed what Philip said and was baptized, but Simon's desire to boast and be revered by people kept him from having a relationship with God. Simon's heart was not aligned with God. All it took to make things right was a conversation that began with the words "Please forgive me, Lord." Sin and bitterness keep us from truly experiencing the love God has for each of us. By repenting, we humble ourselves and draw closer to God. In return, he faithfully draws near to us.[24]

"I can never escape from your Spirit! I can never get away from your presence!" (Psalm 139:7). The bottom line is *we need the Holy Spirit!* "But it was to us that

---

23. "When Simon saw that the Spirit was given when the apostles laid their hands on people, he offered them money to buy this power. 'Let me have this power, too,' he exclaimed, 'so that when I lay my hands on people, they will receive the Holy Spirit!' But Peter replied, 'May your money be destroyed with you for thinking God's gift can be bought! You can have no part in this, for your heart is not right with God. Repent of your wickedness and pray to the Lord. Perhaps he will forgive your evil thoughts, for I can see that you are full of bitter jealousy and are held captive by sin'" (Acts 8:18–23).
24. "So humble yourselves before God. Resist the devil, and he will flee from you. Come close to God, and God will come close to you. Wash your hands, you sinners; purify your hearts, for your loyalty is divided between God and the world" (James 4:7–8).

God revealed these things by his Spirit. For his Spirit searches out everything and shows us God's deep secrets. No one can know a person's thoughts except that person's own spirit, and no one can know God's thoughts except God's own Spirit. And we have received God's Spirit (not the world's spirit), so we can know the wonderful things God has freely given us" (1 Corinthians 2:10–12). Jesus needed the Holy Spirit and so do we.

It's important that I share the Holy Spirit with you. Understanding who he is and why he is important will determine how you receive the remaining chapters of this book. Jesus alone is not the fullness of the gospel just like water baptism is not the fullness of baptism. Many early followers of Jesus only heard half the message. In Acts 19, Paul encountered twelve men who believed what they heard about Jesus and were baptized in water to wash away their sins. None of them knew about the Holy Spirit. Isn't it interesting the first thing Paul asks these disciples is if they received the Holy Spirit when they believed (Acts 19:2)? They hadn't *heard* of him so Paul laid hands on the men and introduced them to the Holy Spirit. This is a part of making disciples. If you are a believer in Jesus, I ask you now, "Did you receive the Holy Spirit when you believed?"[25]

> *"Our heavenly Father, may the glory of your name be the center on which our life turns. May your Holy Spirit come upon us and cleanse us. Manifest your kingdom on earth. And give us our needed bread for the coming day. Forgive our sins as we ourselves release forgiveness to those who have wronged us. And rescue us every time we face tribulations" (Luke 11:2–4 TPT). Prepare our hearts to receive the Holy Spirit and all he is going to teach us. Thank you for this gift and companion. He is the best friend we have, and we are grateful. I lift up to you everyone reading this prayer and*

---

25. "'Did you receive the Holy Spirit when you believed?' he asked them. 'No,' they replied, 'we haven't even heard that there is a Holy Spirit'" (Acts 19:2).

agreeing with me. I ask for the Holy Spirit to come upon us now as we read this.

Thank you for doing this for us, Lord! Thank you for loving us enough to send such a precious gift of yourself to live within us and upon us.

Just as Peter and John prayed for the Holy Spirit to come on the people of Samaria, I also pray this for you. God can do anything, and I am trusting him to do this even if I cannot be there to lay hands on you. His hands are already upon you. As we enter the days ahead, I believe it will become crucial for us to ask other disciples, "Did you receive the Holy Spirit when you believed?" May we be willing to share this gift freely with those willing to receive!

CHAPTER 7

Where Do You Bubble?

How do we hear the Holy Spirit's voice? You might think ... in our ears! Ask yourself this question, "Do I have expectations about the way God should speak to me?" Even now, my answer is "Yes!" I desire to hear his voice clearly and from outside my body. I learned quickly that there is not much grace in this type of communication. What do I mean? Let's look at Moses. As I mentioned before, he communed with God face to face as a friend. God gave Moses specific instructions for providing water for the Israelites. The first time, he obeyed completely. "The Lord said to Moses, 'Walk out in front of the people. Take your staff, the one you used when you struck the water of the Nile, and call some of the elders of Israel to join you. I will stand before you on the rock at Mount Sinai. Strike the rock, and water will come gushing out. Then the people will be able to drink.' So Moses struck the rock as he was told, and water gushed out as the elders looked on" (Exodus 17:5–6).

Later, they needed water again, but Moses did not fully obey:

> Moses and Aaron turned away from the people and went to the entrance of the Tabernacle, where they fell face down on the ground. Then the glorious presence of the Lord appeared to them, and the Lord said to Moses, "You and Aaron must take the staff and assemble the entire community. As the people watch, speak to the rock over there, and it will pour out its water. You will provide enough water from the rock to satisfy the whole community and their livestock."
>
> So Moses did as he was told. He took the staff from the place where it was kept

before the Lord. Then he and Aaron summoned the people to come and gather at the rock. "Listen, you rebels!" he shouted. "Must we bring you water from this rock?" Then Moses raised his hand and struck the rock twice with the staff, and water gushed out. So the entire community and their livestock drank their fill. But the Lord said to Moses and Aaron, "Because you did not trust me enough to demonstrate my holiness to the people of Israel, you will not lead them into the land I am giving them!" (Numbers 20:6–12)

Moses started out on the right track but, in his anger, he did not follow the instructions to speak to the rock. Moses knew striking the rock had worked before, but it seems he wasn't sure speaking to the rock would work.

When we don't obey, it tells God we do not trust him to demonstrate his holiness. When we are given clear instructions directly from the mouth of God, he expects us to follow them. Moses's consequence was not getting to enter the land he spent the last forty years contending and interceding for his people to receive. With clear instruction comes great responsibility to obey accurately.

Let's all take a moment and lay down these expectations and repent.

> *Father, please forgive us for trying to put you into a box. Help us learn to be teachable. We lay down any expectations we have of the Creator of the universe and we realign our desires with your desires. You desire relationship with us, and we admit we've been a bit controlling (to say the least). We ask for your forgiveness in Jesus's name. We thank you for your patience and ask for eyes to see and ears to hear by the power of your Holy Spirit. We want to know you more. Thank you for speaking to us all this time and thank you for giving us a new resolve*

*to listen so we hear your instruction
instead of listening to tickle our ears!*

When we encounter the one true God, our entire being (spirit, soul, and body) is affected. No matter what name you use to relate to God, he is true to his character as described in the Scriptures.[1] For example, God doesn't just love, he actually *is* love.[2] He doesn't have to work at being a loving God. He simply *is*. If the fruit of the Spirit is love, joy, peace, patience, kindness, goodness, gentleness, faithfulness, and self-control, then he must be these things.[3] Love, joy, and peace are emotions or feelings. Patience, kindness, goodness, gentleness, and faithfulness are expressions of feelings towards others. Self-control is how feelings, impulses, or desires are restrained.

---

1. "If we are unfaithful, he remains faithful, for he cannot deny who he is" (2 Timothy 2:13).
2. "All who declare that Jesus is the Son of God have God living in them, and they live in God. We know how much God loves us, and we have put our trust in his love. God is love, and all who live in love live in God, and God lives in them" (1 John 4:15–16).
3. "But the Holy Spirit produces this kind of fruit in our lives: love, joy, peace, patience, kindness, goodness, faithfulness, gentleness, and self–control. There is no law against these things!" (Galatians 5:22–23).

The Word says the Holy Spirit produces this fruit in our lives ... meaning we *become* this fruit. Just like with a regular fruit tree, it takes time and attention before we see fruit. Dead places are pruned to make way for new growth. Years may pass before a young fruit tree is mature enough to bear fruit. As we continue our journey with God, our roots grow deeper and our fruit increases in quality and quantity. We become healthy, godly expressions of emotion as the Holy Spirit matures us and produces this fruit in our lives. My purpose here is to dispel the myth that "God is not a feeling" when Scripture clearly describes him as such.[4]

Many times, an intense emotion will cause a physical reaction in our body. Having a physical response to the voice of God is not surprising. Ezekiel fell face down on the ground in God's glory.[5] John also had this experience when Jesus visited him at Patmos to deliver the book of Revelation.[6] Think back to a time where you knew his

---

4. "Dear friends, let us continue to love one another, for love comes from God. Anyone who loves is a child of God and knows God. But anyone who does not love does not know God, for God is love" (1 John 4:7-8).
5. Ezekiel 1:28; 3:22; 9:8; 11:13; 43:2; 44:4.
6. "It was the Lord's Day, and I was worshiping in the Spirit.

presence was in the room. It could be the first time you realized Jesus is truly the Son of God, during a worship service, a time when someone prayed over you, or any number of other instances where you could feel inside your body that God was there. Perhaps you also cried or laughed during that time. Remember in the first chapter where I felt a pull or tugging in my belly when God spoke to me? To this day, that is where he resonates when I ask him things. If the Holy Spirit dwells within you, why is it a surprise that he would speak from a place inside of your body? You are his temple.[7] He chose you! If you do some research on the temple, you will be blessed by it.

Suddenly, I heard behind me a loud voice like a trumpet blast. It said, 'Write in a book everything you see, and send it to the seven churches in the cities of Ephesus, Smyrna, Pergamum, Thyatira, Sardis, Philadelphia, and Laodicea.' ... When I saw him, I fell at his feet as if I were dead. But he laid his right hand on me and said, 'Don't be afraid! I am the First and the Last. I am the living one. I died, but look—I am alive forever and ever! And I hold the keys of death and the grave'" (Revelation 1:10–11,17–18).
7. "Don't you realize that your body is the temple of the Holy Spirit, who lives in you and was given to you by God? You do not belong to yourself, for God bought you with a high price. So you must honor God with your body"
(1 Corinthians 6:19–20).

Jesus says his sheep know his voice.[8] The best place to test whether something you hear is from God is Scripture.[9] In the parable of the good shepherd, Jesus explains how he is the Good Shepherd to his people. Lambs are taught from birth to follow the flock and to recognize the shepherd's voice. You have been God's beloved son or daughter since before you were born. He has been exposing you to his voice and, hopefully, you belong to an amazing flock that hears him and follows him. If not, I encourage you to ask God where to find your people.[10]

While I do not want to spend much time on this topic, I believe it is important to point out that there are voices other than God's that we can hear (even from inside of us). If you don't have a relationship with Jesus, *do not pray in his name or attempt to cast out demons*. Here's why:

---

8. "My sheep listen to my voice; I know them, and they follow me" (John 10:27).
9. "Do not stifle the Holy Spirit. Do not scoff at prophecies, but test everything that is said. Hold on to what is good. Stay away from every kind of evil" (1 Thessalonians 5:19–22).
10. John 10

A group of Jews was traveling from town to town casting out evil spirits. They tried to use the name of the Lord Jesus in their incantation, saying, "I command you in the name of Jesus, whom Paul preaches, to come out!" Seven sons of Sceva, a leading priest, were doing this. But one time when they tried it, the evil spirit replied, "I know Jesus, and I know Paul, but who are you?" Then the man with the evil spirit leaped on them, overpowered them, and attacked them with such violence that they fled from the house, naked and battered. The story of what happened spread quickly all through Ephesus, to Jews and Greeks alike. A solemn fear descended on the city, and the name of the Lord Jesus was greatly honored. (Acts 19:13–17)

Here is a sample prayer we use to silence demonic voices, so we know the *only* voice we are hearing is the Holy Spirit:

> *Father, we take authority over and bind anything demonic within us and around us in the name of Jesus. We cast them to the feet of Jesus. We say to all voices that are not God, "Silence and go!" To anything remaining, we say, "The Lord rebuke you." We ask the shed blood of Jesus to be over us and an angel guard to protect us. All this we ask in the name of Jesus and by the power of your Holy Spirit.*

In Luke 11:13, Jesus said if we, being evil, know how to give good gifts to our children, how much *more* will the Father give the Holy Spirit to those who ask! This assures us, when we seek God and listen for his voice, he will not send a demonic voice to answer us. He's a good Father and gives the Holy Spirit when we ask.

"Jesus replied, 'Anyone who drinks this water will soon become thirsty again. But those who drink the water I give will never be thirsty again. It becomes a fresh, bubbling spring within them, giving them eternal life'"

(John 4:13–14). Jesus also said, "Anyone who believes in me may come and drink! For the Scriptures declare, 'Rivers of living water will flow from his heart.' (When he said 'living water,' he was speaking of the Spirit, who would be given to everyone believing in him. But the Spirit had not yet been given, because Jesus had not yet entered into his glory)" (John 7:38–39). Jesus entered into his glory when he fulfilled his assignment on the earth through his death on the cross.

> As they talked and discussed these things with each other, Jesus himself came up and walked along with them; but they were kept from recognizing him.
>
> He asked them, "What are you discussing together as you walk along?"
>
> They stood still, their faces downcast. ...
>
> He said to them, "How foolish you are, and how slow to believe all that the prophets have spoken! Did not the

> Messiah have to suffer these things and then enter his glory?" And beginning with Moses and all the Prophets, he explained to them what was said in all the Scriptures concerning himself. (Luke 24:15–17, 25–27 NIV)

Jesus entered his glory and sent us the Holy Spirit who bubbles like a refreshing spring within us. Where do you bubble? In what part of your body do you feel living waters bubbling up? On the day of Pentecost in Acts 2:16–21, Peter explains this outpouring of the Holy Spirit:

> What you see was predicted long ago by the prophet Joel: "In the last days," God says, "I will pour out my Spirit upon all people. Your sons and daughters will prophesy. Your young men will see visions, and your old men will dream dreams. In those days I will pour out my Spirit even on my servants—men and women alike—and they will prophesy.

And I will cause wonders in the heavens above and signs on the earth below—blood and fire and clouds of smoke. The sun will become dark, and the moon will turn blood red before that great and glorious day of the Lord arrives. But everyone who calls on the name of the Lord will be saved."

We are living in this time as God continues to pour out the Holy Spirit on new believer after new believer. The four blood moons of 2015 testify that God is *still* pouring out his Spirit. All of creation testifies to the glory of God, and he continues to confirm that the Holy Spirit is living in his people to this day.[11] God doesn't need to turn the moon red to remind himself to send the Holy Spirit to his believers. He continues to perform these signs and wonders because *we* need to be reminded that we need the Holy Spirit. What a terrible God he would be if he gave the Holy Spirit and the gifts of the Spirit for

---

11. "For ever since the world was created, people have seen the earth and sky. Through everything God made, they can clearly see his invisible qualities—his eternal power and divine nature. So they have no excuse for not knowing God" (Romans 1:20).

the first hundred years after Jesus and then removed them from the earth![12] The world has not gotten any better. We have the same enemy they had, and I cannot believe that God would withdraw a gift he intended for *all* people.[13] With God, all means all.

Jesus said, "I also tell you this: If two of you agree here on earth concerning anything you ask, my Father in heaven will do it for you. For where two or three gather together in my name. I am there among them" (Matthew 18:19–20). Find a partner and a quiet place. Let's ask our Father: "Will you pour out your Spirit on us and bubble within us so we can learn where you like to speak to us?" Pay attention to your body. Does one area "light up"? This could be anywhere from your head to your toes. If you tend to analyze things, pay attention to your mind. My husband experiences the Holy Spirit in this way. A section in his brain becomes active when God is speaking to him. I am a "feeler"[14] so my belly is where

---

12. "The Lord is good to everyone. He showers compassion on all his creation" (Psalm 145:9).
13. "For we are not fighting against flesh-and-blood enemies, but against evil rulers and authorities of the unseen world, against mighty powers in this dark world, and against evil spirits in the heavenly places" (Ephesians 6:12).

he bubbles. Wait for him. Be like the 120 who listened to the words of Jesus and waited for God to send his Spirit on those in the upper room in Acts 2. He is faithful to bubble! May I pray with you?

> *Father, may we have more of your Holy Spirit, please? You said that if we ask, you would give us more of this wonderful gift. We ask in the name of your Son, Jesus, and by the power of your Holy Spirit. Come quickly! Would you pour your Spirit out on us as we read this prayer? I also ask that you bubble within each person reading this and witness with their spirit. May the Holy Spirit within them burn and confirm all that you are saying and doing through this book. We receive you and welcome you in Jesus's name. Thank You for this gift of your Holy Spirit. There is no greater gift and there is nothing we have needed more than you!*

---

14. Taken from Prophetic Personalities Course: https://shop.truthtotable.com/collections/digital-courses-studies/products/prophetic-personalities-course.

CHAPTER 8

Practice: Asking Questions and the Holy Spirit Game

I love to ask questions. I remember one night when I was little. My mom drove us home. I was asking a thousand questions like "Why is the sky blue?" and "Who created God?" All I remember her saying was, "I don't know." I finally looked at her and said, "You're a mom ... you're supposed to know everything!" I really thought she knew everything. I was shocked to find out she didn't. That night was also the first time I ever saw a shooting star. I remember it like it was yesterday.

Why am I telling you this? Once I realized the people around me didn't have answers, I began to wonder to myself about them. I have a thing for details. I notice things around me and suddenly ask questions about them to whomever is nearby. Now I'm a mom to three inquisitive boys and realize how impossible it is to know everything.

After learning that God talks to me, I began feeling that place in my belly bubble up often as I thought about things. I learned this meant he wanted me to explore further.[1] I asked him about what classes I should take, sports to play, career path to take, and college to attend. I started with the big stuff—the major life decisions. He was faithful to respond. Additionally, I felt knots or downward tugs when I was around dangerous situations, people, and places under a demonic influence. I believe this was the beginning of discernment and may be a survival mechanism for a new believer. Just like babies can tell if the person holding them is capable and competent, young believers may have a heightened

---

1. "Keep on asking, and you will receive what you ask for. Keep on seeking, and you will find. Keep on knocking, and the door will be opened to you. For everyone who asks, receives. Everyone who seeks, finds. And to everyone who knocks, the door will be opened" (Matthew 7:7–8).

spiritual sensitivity to avoid spiritually dangerous situations.

In 2017, I had an opportunity to substitute teach for our church's private school. When I asked the students if they thought God spoke to them, nearly 100 percent answered, "No." This grieved me because I knew they thought God didn't care about them or they were in some way unworthy of him. Do you feel like this sometimes? You've made some bad decisions and done some horrible things. You wonder deep down if God would even *want* to talk to you. Let me share a little truth that encourages me when those condemning thoughts arise. God desires to speak with you *more* than you desire to hear his voice. He cares about the tears that you cry,[2] the hairs on your head,[3] and, most of all, the desires of your heart.[4] He planted many of those desires and wants to see them fulfilled *even more* than you do!

---

2. "You keep track of all my sorrows. You have collected all my tears in your bottle. You have recorded each one in your book" (Psalm 56:8).
3. "And the very hairs on your head are all numbered. So don't be afraid; you are more valuable to God than a whole flock of sparrows" (Matthew 10:30–31).
4. "Take delight in the Lord, and he will give you your heart's desires" (Psalm 37:4).

God began showing me ways to help teens recognize when they hear his voice. He gave me something we like to call the "Holy Spirit Game." We started with yes and no questions. There's a fifty percent chance we'll hear correctly. I would know the answer to the question, and they would ask the Holy Spirit for the answer. Many students found they heard the answer. Others tended to guess instead of asking the Holy Spirit. I encouraged them to sit still for a few seconds to wait on the answer. We quickly moved to asking open-ended questions like colors and numbers. "What's my favorite color?" or "What number am I thinking of?" It seems silly, but he answered our questions The students (and I) gained confidence through this Holy Spirit training. Then the questions changed again to something like, "What do you want to tell me about that person?" We asked about each other or people in our lives and would pray what he was saying.

One student took this game home and taught her family at their weekly game night. Her stepdad was skeptical. He couldn't believe God was answering these types of questions. His stepdaughter thought of the color red. He prayed, "If you are really answering these questions, Holy Spirit, tell me the color she is thinking of." He saw a flash of red and took a risk by answering. He was shocked. God cared enough about the condition of her stepdad's heart to answer the question!

As we grow more familiar with his voice and where he speaks, we don't have to keep asking if it is God. We know and now we take the risk that when we ask and hear an answer, it is the Holy Spirit. Remember, his sheep hear his voice! He wants us to practice listening and using our gifts.[5] God desires to hear about everything in our lives.[6] He wants us to talk to him and have conversation with him!

---

5. "Do not neglect the gift you have, which was given you by prophecy when the council of elders laid their hands on you. Practice these things, immerse yourself in them, so that all may see your progress" (1 Timothy 4:14–15 ESV).
6. "Don't be pulled in different directions or worried about a thing. Be saturated in prayer throughout each day, offering your faith-filled requests before God with overflowing gratitude. Tell him every detail of your life, then God's wonderful peace that transcends human understanding, will make the answers known to you through Jesus Christ" (Philippians 4:6–7 TPT).

The next step is to begin asking God about other people. He may give you names, birthdates, hurts, fears, or just a feeling of his love for them. Be prepared to pray for these people. We're not asking about them just to gather information. We ask the Holy Spirit about the people around us so we can pray for them, share with them, and see them through God's eyes. Please do not limit God to only these ways of communicating. Let him share with you whatever his heart desires, however he desires.

My point is that God wants us to hear his voice clearly so we can speak his Word clearly to connect that person back to him. Below are just two (of many) examples of when God delivered details to people in the Bible that changed the course of history. An Old Testament example can be found in 1 Samuel 10:1–7 (NIV):

> Then Samuel took a flask of olive oil and poured it on Saul's head and kissed him, saying, "Has not the Lord anointed you ruler over his inheritance? When you leave me today, you will meet two men near Rachel's tomb, at Zelzah on the border of

Benjamin. They will say to you, 'The donkeys you set out to look for have been found. And now your father has stopped thinking about them and is worried about you. He is asking, "What shall I do about my son?"'

"Then you will go on from there until you reach the great tree of Tabor. Three men going up to worship God at Bethel will meet you there. One will be carrying three young goats, another three loaves of bread, and another a skin of wine. They will greet you and offer you two loaves of bread, which you will accept from them.

"After that you will go to Gibeah of God, where there is a Philistine outpost. As you approach the town, you will meet a procession of prophets coming down from the high place with lyres, timbrels, pipes and harps being played before them, and they will be prophesying. The Spirit of the

Lord will come powerfully upon you, and you will prophesy with them; and you will be changed into a different person. Once these signs are fulfilled, do whatever your hand finds to do, for God is with you."

A New Testament example is found in Acts 9:10–19:

> In Damascus there was a disciple named Ananias. The Lord called to him in a vision, "Ananias!"
>
> "Yes, Lord," he answered.
>
> The Lord told him, "Go to the house of Judas on Straight Street and ask for a man from Tarsus named Saul, for he is praying. In a vision he has seen a man named Ananias come and place his hands on him to restore his sight."
>
> "Lord," Ananias answered, "I have heard many reports about this man and all the

harm he has done to your holy people in Jerusalem. And he has come here with authority from the chief priests to arrest all who call on your name."

But the Lord said to Ananias, "Go! This man is my chosen instrument to proclaim my name to the Gentiles and their kings and to the people of Israel. I will show him how much he must suffer for my name."

Then Ananias went to the house and entered it. Placing his hands on Saul, he said, "Brother Saul, the Lord—Jesus, who appeared to you on the road as you were coming here—has sent me so that you may see again and be filled with the Holy Spirit." Immediately, something like scales fell from Saul's eyes, and he could see again. He got up and was baptized, and after taking some food, he regained his strength.

> Saul spent several days with the disciples in Damascus.

God answered all possible questions in this passage: Who? What? When? Where? How? and Why? We see details like street names and God sharing other people's thoughts and feelings. He also shared their future. If he'll do it for them, he'll do it for us![7]

> For Jesus Christ, the Son of God, does not waver between "Yes" and "No." He is the one whom Silas, Timothy, and I preached to you, and as God's ultimate "Yes," he always does what he says. For all of God's promises have been fulfilled in Christ with a resounding "Yes!" And through Christ, our "Amen" (which means "Yes") ascends to God for his glory.

> It is God who enables us, along with you, to stand firm for Christ. He has

---

[7]. "God is not a man, so he does not lie. He is not human, so he does not change his mind. Has he ever spoken and failed to act? Has he ever promised and not carried it through?" (Numbers 23:19)

commissioned us, and he has identified us as his own by placing the Holy Spirit in our hearts as the first installment that guarantees everything he has promised us." (2 Corinthians 1:19–22)

God knows us intimately and he desires for us to experience him deeply. It's not enough to identify stories about him. Time to go deeper! We practice all kinds of things. Let's practice communicating with the Holy Spirit so we can walk by him at all times, doing what we see the Father doing and saying what we hear the Father saying. Grab a friend (or your kids!) and go play the Holy Spirit game. We do this often, so we don't get bogged down in trying to hear him. Your mindset relaxes when you are playing a game. Take the risk, you'll be glad you did!

CHAPTER 9

The Rest of My Story

In the fifth grade, I knew God wanted me to play the flute and become a band director. I told my mom about my desire to join band, and she shared this with my dad. For our family, it was a big investment to buy a musical instrument. My dad was concerned I would not stick with band. I believe God convinced my dad to purchase the flute for me so he could share in the glory that God was receiving through my obedience.

As a teenager, I began to hear people's thoughts. That was the only way I knew to describe it. They were so clear and in that person's voice. I would respond to them as if they had spoken to me. I truly thought they were saying these things out loud until a friend said, "How did you know what I was thinking?" Once I realized what was happening, I wrote to God about it. I knew it was a gift from him (known as words of knowledge and burden bearing).[1] I asked him how to develop this gift for his glory. I never really heard much more from God regarding this gift. After a few years, I thought he took it away because I hadn't experienced it in a long time. Through healing courses and counseling, I discovered I blocked it because of different choices and sin in my life. I would have misused it like Simon the sorcerer we spoke of earlier. But God was gracious to me during that time.

In 1996, at the age of twelve, I began writing down dreams. I didn't know God spoke through dreams, but I did like to write and thought they would make a great story to read later. Nobody was talking about the prophetic gifts (church-speak for "hearing God"): words of wisdom, words of knowledge, and those types of gifts.

---

1. "A spiritual gift is given to each of us so we can help each other. To one person the Spirit gives the ability to give wise advice; to another the same Spirit gives a message of special knowledge" (1 Corinthians 12:7–8).

Needless to say, I stifled this gift for a while. A dear friend who studied astrology and the zodiac introduced me to some dream interpretation books. The information was vague and didn't satisfy my curiosity. I was (and still am) interested more in personal details, not generalities.

Also, when I was twelve, I wrote a letter to God about the kind of man I wanted to marry. It contained details like body structure, eye color, hair color, and different personality traits I found attractive. I also expressed in this letter that my dream car was a Dodge Neon. I poured out all of these things in my heart to God. I never spoke to him about them again, but something happened when I wrote that letter. I remember laying it on my window sill expecting it to be gone the next morning because an angel delivered it to God. It never left the ledge. Over the years, God answered every single one of these requests, and I wish I had a copy to share with you. He later told me that there is anointing in the hand. There is something special when we put pencil to paper and pour out our hearts to God.

In 1999, at age fifteen I met my husband and he met every single desire I laid out in my letter except the eye color. I asked for gray eyes, but Shawn's are green. That's pretty close if you ask me! I thought that was a pretty good compromise, and that God just overlooked that request. How little I knew God! In 2013, he reminded me of how I worded the request. I thought I was talking about my husband when I wrote, "I'd like *a guy* with gray eyes." He gave me "a guy" with gray eyes in my sweet firstborn son in 2012.

God cares about the desires of our hearts (even our completely self-centered twelve-year-old desires). This is the Father's heart. If you're a parent, you know what I mean. You want to give your children everything their little hearts desire, but you also understand that everything they want is not always good for them. As a parent, you know what is best for your children. God is the same way. He has gone before you and knows every day of your life. He knows what will benefit you and what will harm you. It's a mercy of the Lord to withhold a desire of our heart if it will harm us. This is where we trust and obey even if we don't understand. Lay your desires at his feet and watch him love on you.

In high school, I felt an urge from the Lord to explore intercessory prayer. This is prayer on behalf of others. I sought out the prayer ministry leader in our church and tried to get more information. He didn't seem too interested in helping me so I did what I could. I attended a few of their intercessory prayer meetings, but soon God told me not to go anymore. He began waking me up around 3 o'clock in the morning, teaching me to pray. Like Samuel, I heard my name called in the middle of the night.[2] I answered the Lord for many years. I also started dancing for God on the worship team at this church. That was the best experience, and I still love to dance for the Lord to this day.

The summer before I started college, my sister tried to catch my brother-in-law, Ronnie, as he was having a seizure-like attack after getting too hot outside. They weren't seizures, and doctors had no name for them, so

---

2. "So the Lord called a third time, and once more Samuel got up and went to Eli. 'Here I am. Did you call me?' Then Eli realized it was the Lord who was calling the boy" (1 Samuel 3:8).

we called them "attacks." His hands would lock up and he was not able to respond. Every muscle in his body became rigid, making his body heavy when he fell. My sister, Alana, hurt her back so badly she had to have subsequent surgeries and became permanently disabled. This put a financial strain on my mom because now they were down to one income. It took a long time for my sister to get disability pay because she was in her mid-thirties. The three of them lived together along with my nephew in Mom's house.

I followed my husband to Georgia Southern University to study music education. This is when God gave me a supernatural faith for healing. Before one of my symphony performances, I received a call from my sister. She and my brother-in-law were in a car accident. Ronnie broke his sternum and bruised many ribs. As she spoke, I felt a fire come over my body as I realized this accident was an attack by the enemy. "The thief's [Satan's] purpose is to steal and kill and destroy. My purpose is to give them a rich and satisfying life" (John 10:10). I was angry at the enemy. Sitting on the steps in a dark alley behind the music building, I told Alana to place her hand on Ronnie's chest. I prayed over the phone. Later that night my brother-in-law tried to check himself out of the hospital. He no longer felt pain. They took another X-ray, and found his sternum was no longer cracked. God healed him! I believed God for healing miracles. I just hadn't witnessed it or had him use me to bring healing to others. Years later, I would experience my own supernatural healing.

My college years were a dark period. I struggled with anxiety, depression, and various other health issues. Adjustment to life away from home was difficult. However, I experienced very little drama. So why was life so hard? Codependency. I hated the chaos and uncertainty, but I didn't know how to live without it. I was sensitive to things happening back home.

I got married in my second year of college. The pressure to perform as a musician was enough to break anyone. I had chosen one of the most difficult degrees available. I consider this period dark because my relationship with God did not move forward. I longed to progress and go deeper, but I couldn't figure out how to juggle all of this new responsibility. God patiently waited for me. He was sweet to me as I struggled to survive this season.

After graduation in 2008, my life purpose was fulfilled as I took a band director position in a small town close to home. Everything I had been working toward was finally coming to fruition. I regularly made music and my career a priority over people. The school system I worked for claimed to be a public school that loved Jesus. Almost all of the staff believed in God. We prayed before every event despite laws removing prayer from public schools.

I would later find out they were only Christ-followers in word, not deed. Until then, I poured my life into the students and music program. My first year was great. The parents gave me a lot of grace as an outsider to their small community. The students were wonderful. I still love them to this day, and my life will forever be changed because of them. I truly thought I would retire from that school. It was a dream come true to be in a school where I could share my faith and my passion for music. It didn't last long, though.

I felt a nudge from God in my second year. There were many warnings, and I knew I was on my way out. The parents were complaining more. Things began to heat up. Not only that, but the administration stretched me across three schools. By the end of my second year, I was teaching elementary, middle, and high school music. Before my third year, they cut my beginning band program and opted for general music. In an effort to keep alive the program I had built, I opted for no breaks during the day. I added extra practices and enlisted my high schoolers to help me start beginning band students. It was hard, long, and it nearly killed me ... at least that's how it felt. I was sick many times that year.

In October of 2010, the band booster parents accused me of stealing from the booster club, among other things. I was shocked. What they didn't know was that I had paid two of their bills (over a thousand dollars) that summer with my own money. Not to mention the instruments, supplies, and food I bought throughout the years there. A large meeting was called, and my principal told all of the parents and their kids that I did not put money in the proper account (school or booster club bank accounts), and that he would make sure I never did that again. Besides the fact there wasn't a guideline about which monies went into which account, my principal prided himself on being on the teachers' side when it came to parents. Even if we were in the wrong, he would support us to the parents, and reprimand us in private ... or so we thought. That was the beginning of the end for my band career.

A few months earlier, my niece lost her husband suddenly. He passed while away at his mom's. My sister, Alana, was in remission from multiple sclerosis (MS) at the time. She planned to help my niece with her kids over the holidays. Alana went to be with them from Thanksgiving to early January 2011. My mom and brother-in-law were home for the holidays. Shawn and I celebrated with them.

January 2011 proved to be the most difficult month of my life. That sounds extreme, but I assure you this is the truth. In twenty-four hours, I faced my two deepest fears. On January 14, my high school band class was rehearsing a march for Large Group Performance

Evaluation (LGPE). This was the first year they would participate, and we were required to do a march. Rehearsal was going great. It was the final class of the day. The students were listening to every word I said. They made the stylistic changes I suggested and were sounding fantastic. I was beginning to think we might achieve the highest mark of Superior if we kept up this pace.

I heard a knock on the door. The assistant principal poked his head in and motioned for me to step out into the hallway. The principal wanted to see me in his office. I was a little nervous because of the problems with parents from October. I swallowed hard and made the short walk around the corner to the front office. When I walked in, I was shocked to also see our superintendent, the head of our local school system. He determined who stayed and who went. Now I was really nervous. They asked me to sit down and I complied. The events of the last few months ran through my mind. *What did I do now? I can't seem to catch a break. I hope they have good news.*

The superintendent spoke first. "We've called you here today to let you know we aren't going to be able to renew your teaching contract for next year." My heart sank. Funding for music programs was being cut all over the country. Because of the economic situation in our country, I began my job as a band director fearing I would lose it. Now that fear became a reality. This was pretty much like getting fired but having to work the next four months like nothing happened. I had to finish the school year and would have to disclose on future teaching applications that my contract was not renewed. It isn't as bad as having a criminal record, but pretty close.

Pull yourself together, Tiffany. Don't let them see you cry! I was able to hold back the sobs, and finally mustered the strength to say, "Do you mind if I ask why?"

He said, "People haven't been pleased with the direction the program was going, and they haven't seen enough growth."

I was stunned. *What people? The administration? How did I miss this? The parents weren't happy with me, but I have been bending over backwards to please them.* I finally pulled myself together and said, "Were you not pleased with our growth and direction? At the end of each year, I met with you and discussed the goals we completed, the ones we didn't, and plans for the following year. You never once mentioned anything was wrong."

The administrators sat quietly. They couldn't bring themselves to look me in the eye. I anxiously awaited their response. Finally, my principal spoke up. "We cannot discuss any of the details."

I knew then what they were doing was illegal. I was stuck. I could fight and be investigated (which requires disclosure on future applications as well) or take the hit of the nonrenewal and pray that God would give me favor. I chose the nonrenewal. *What will happen now? On* every *teaching application, I have to disclose I didn't have my contract renewed.* As all of these thoughts were crashing around inside my mind, I managed to make it through the entire meeting without shedding a single tear. I pulled myself together, looked squarely at them, and asked, "Is there anything else we need to discuss?" Sheepishly looking down at his hands ... "No, we're all done here," my principal said.

I rose from my seat and prepared to face my students. I still had thirty minutes of class to teach. My heart was broken. I arrived at the door to my classroom. How was I going to hide my emotions from them? I took a few deep breaths and opened the door. My assistant principal met me at the door. I thanked him for watching my class. He saw I was upset and gave a sympathetic half-hearted smile to say, "you're welcome." Right after he left, one of my sensitive students with a form of high-functioning autism spectrum disorder could see I was upset. I couldn't lie to him because he was working on identifying emotions and responding appropriately. I didn't want to confuse him. He made great progress in my music class. It was important for me to be truthful, stay strong, and finish the day. He asked over and over if I was all right. He vocalized what everyone else was thinking. I explained I had gotten some bad news, but everything was going to be okay. It had upset me, and it's okay to have that feeling.

We began rehearsing again, and tears streamed down my face. I was doing all I could to hold back the sobs. *How do they expect me to finish out the day much less the rest of the year? I don't think I can do this.* Then I suddenly remembered I had to judge vocal auditions right after school. *Could this day get any worse?*

Finally, class was over, and all of my students were sitting and talking. I could tell they were concerned, but I couldn't tell them anything yet. Later, while I was in the music room waiting on the auditions, one of my seniors said, "Mrs. Downs, why are you so upset? The students are really worried about you." I wrestled with whether or not to tell her what happened. I finally decided it would be okay. She was mature and trustworthy. I explained I got fired, and how that works for teachers. I told her she couldn't tell anyone. I wanted to wait before I announced it to all of my students.

I managed to get through the auditions. I hopped into my beat-up red Dodge Neon and made the three-minute drive home. When I pulled into the driveway at six o'clock, the first thing I did was call my mom. She picked up and I lost it. I cried so hard I could barely breathe. My mom got my sister, Alana, on the phone too. I hadn't seen my sister since before Thanksgiving when she left to help take care of her grandchildren. I told them every last detail. My mom was livid. She was quiet for most of the conversation. The only thing I remember her saying was, "I am very upset that they did that to you." Her voice was so calculated. I could tell she was forcing herself to remain calm. I sat in the driveway for about thirty minutes talking to them before my husband walked out on the front porch. He motioned supper was ready. I told my mom and sister I loved them and would see them the following day. I planned to go to work with mom in the morning to help her. She said I didn't have to, but I told her I didn't mind. We decided that if she needed me, she would call.

I walked inside and everyone was at the table. A childhood friend, his wife, and their two precious boys lived with us. They moved from the Midwest in August to go back to school. We were glad to help them. They took one look at my face and immediately knew something was wrong. I explained everything that transpired that day ... every last detail. After we had our emotional outbursts and settled, our next step was to figure out what to do from here. I decided to sleep on it, and we would come up with a plan tomorrow.

When I woke up the next morning, I got ready to go to the post office. At nine o'clock, I got a phone call from the Sports Hall of Fame where Mom worked. I answered the phone. Her boss said, "Have you heard from your mom this morning? She hasn't made it to work." Fear immediately gripped me. Something was wrong. Mom had been working seven days a week for nearly seven years and had *never* once been late ... *never*! I gathered my thoughts and said, "I will give her a call and let you know. I'm sure she just overslept."

My husband could tell something was wrong. I said, "That was Ben from Sports. Mom hasn't made it to work yet. I'm going to call her now and find out where she is."

I called her cell phone ... no answer. I dialed the house phone ... no answer. Next, I tried Alana's and Ronnie's cell phones ... no answer. Shawn offered to call his sister, who lived less than ten minutes away, to ask her to go check on them. I agreed this would be the best option. I was trying not to panic. In a matter-of-fact voice, I said, "I am going to the post office. When I return, I expect that Mom will have simply overslept." I left knowing something more was going on.

I prayed the entire way to the post office. Sitting in the parking lot, I remember asking God, "What is going on?" Little did I know he was about to show me. I stepped out of the car and immediately saw a picture in my mind. Alana, Ronnie, and Mom were lying on the floor, passed out behind their couch. I had never had a vision from God before, so I just thought my imagination was getting the best of me. I mailed the package and headed back home.

When I walked inside the house, the atmosphere was frantic. My sister-in-law had arrived at my Mom's and reported back. The door was locked so she had to use the key above the door. Shawn said, "We gotta go! I'll tell you in the car." We had an hour-long drive ahead of us. I was really afraid now.

We arrived to find Mom and Alana dead at the scene, but my brother-in-law, Ronnie, was still alive and transported to the hospital. Because all three had been shot in the head, they checked his hands for gunshot residue. Ronnie lived for three days without any assistance. I could see tears streaming down his face at different times, but he never woke up. Later, we discovered there was gunshot residue on his hands. This was my absolute deepest fear. I recalled from childhood fearing my mom's death. I would regularly cry myself to sleep thinking about her dying. Here we were ... at *that* moment.

A twenty-four-hour whirlwind changed the entire course of my life. I thought my relationship with God was great before all of this. I remember crying for the first day or two after they died and no more after that for the next year. I spent the next eight months in my bedroom. I would come out for food sometimes, then go right back.

I resisted taking medication because I thought people would think my faith in God was weak. It took me eight months to get to the end of myself. I needed help to get out of this pit.

The only sane thought I held on to for months was Romans 8:28: "And we know that God causes everything to work together for the good of those who love God and are called according to his purpose for them." I knew God couldn't lie and I knew I loved him. I would tell him often I didn't know *how* he was going to make it work for my good, but I knew he would do it. A dear friend told me once that sometimes we mourn things before they come because when it happens, we might not have time or strength in the moment. It seems that I spent all of my life (ages three to twenty-seven) mourning my mom's death.

As a result of the murders, I was granted short-term disability through my insurance so I could recover. I didn't have to go back to teaching right away. That was a blessing. In March of that year, the insurance company wanted me to try to go back to work. I can only imagine how I must have looked. My colleagues had shocked looks on their faces, and they seemed nervous around me. I made it half a day, and the elementary principal came into my class and sat down. I was nervous having her in there because I thought she was evaluating me. I tried to go the next day, but after the first period, I had to leave. I went to the principal's office to inform them I was going home. The assistant principal who relieved me the day I was fired was the only administrator in the office. I sat down to talk to him. He had no idea they were giving me such bad news when he came to get me that day. He apologized profusely and was concerned I was upset with him. I assured him I wasn't. We had a great conversation.

I went home for the next two months. I wanted to say goodbye to my students, so I returned for the last week of classes. That weekend, Shawn's brother was in a fatal car accident. He died four months to the day after my family. We were working on a children's book together before he passed.

After these traumatic deaths in the family and a career shift from band director to housewife, I really began to talk to the Lord. I complained every single day about house work. I knew how to be a workaholic with three jobs outside the home. I hated doing dishes, laundry, and anything else that required cleaning. That was a problem since my new job was *housewife*. I had no idea how to make a house a home! I wrestled with God and finally had a temper tantrum in the laundry room. I told him if he wanted me to do this job, he was going to have to change my heart because I hated his calling at this time. I found no joy at all in this new role. I knew this stemmed from heart wounds from my childhood.

During this time, I was advised to ask God what my husband needed done for the day. I realized then God answers the little questions. Once, he told me to do the dishes even though the living room was a wreck (and I wanted to clean the living room). God knew Shawn would come in and put his coffee cup down in the sink right when he walked in the door. This helped me to enjoy the work because now I didn't feel I had to do everything all at once. God began healing my heart and gave me such joy as time progressed.

I developed a regular time dedicated to God in this season. When I became a mom in 2012, I no longer had the freedom to commune with God the way I had before—or so I thought. I learned to adjust with the season. Because I knew I couldn't go years without God's company like I did in college, I asked him how I needed to adjust. Naptimes became sacred times with God. He began to give me revelation about Scripture. I saw more pictures (visions) as I read and worshipped.

I once heard someone say on the radio that God didn't care about what clothes we wore. At the time, I was asking him every day what to wear because he knew what my husband liked the most. The Holy Spirit has picked out every single piece of clothing in my closet, and I regularly ask him what to put on each morning. He knows what's in store for me throughout the day so why not ask him what I might need!

When we bought our home in Florida, we remodeled an abandoned property. Everyone in the neighborhood was curious about who was fixing up the house that had been rotting for almost ten years. They would sometimes look in the windows.

There was a large plant by the front door. I remember wondering what type it was. I knew there was no way for me to find out on my own because I don't know anything about plants! I had nowhere to start. I didn't even really ask God about the plant. I thought about it for a second and moved on with my day.

The next day, a lady walked onto our porch and looked in the front window. I opened the front door and introduced myself. Her sweet mom was there, and we started talking. She proceeded to tell me all about the plant. I never once asked her about it. She told me about how snakes love to live in it, and I should just chop it down now. She told me the proper name (which I can't recall now) and other details that only someone who gardens would know!

It's these types of encounters that help me know beyond a shadow of a doubt God hears me and he cares about what I care about! I pray that you never lose your "wonder." If you feel you've already lost it, begin looking at things like a child discovering the world for the first time. Begin wondering again!

I have countless stories similar to the one above. God continues to blow me away with how much he cares for me. I mistakenly found my identity in my job as a band director and in my mom. I'm not saying God had to remove them so I could find myself in him, but I am glad he did. It was merciful to take my mom before she retired. A career is just an assignment, not a purpose. Our purpose is in Romans 8:29–30, "For God knew his people in advance, and he chose them to become like his Son, so that his Son would be the firstborn among many brothers and sisters. And having chosen them, he called them to come to him. And having called them, he gave them right standing with himself. And having given them right standing, he gave them his glory." No matter what I do or where I may be, I am to become like Jesus, the Son of God, and so are you! Thank you for taking this journey with me and for remaining to the end!

A final prayer for you:

> *Father God, bless all the people who read these words. Increase their capacity to love your people. Give them fresh vision and direction. Answer their small questions ... the ones that really matter to them! Show them your glory and give them peace. I thank you for each and every one. Do what only you can do in their life! I ask these things in Jesus's name and thank you for them.*

APPENDIX A

Relationship with Jesus

All it takes is: "If you declare with your mouth, 'Jesus is Lord,' and believe in your heart that God raised him from the dead, you will be saved. For it is with your heart that you believe and are justified, and it is with your mouth that you profess your faith and are saved" (Romans 10:9–10). You can do this right now! You don't need a special prayer, but if you'd like something to get you started, you can use this one:

> *Jesus, I believe that you really are the Son of God. I believe you died just for me and that God raised you from the dead three days later. Jesus, please forgive me for* (be specific and ask God to forgive you for

anything that comes to mind. No need to feel shame here. God is washing you clean by the blood of his Son. Once you confess to him, it is forgiven ... forever! Let the tears fall freely and be healed.) *I ask for the Holy Spirit in the name of Jesus. The Spirit of God who raised Jesus from the dead lives in* (insert your name here). *And just as God raised Christ Jesus from the dead, he will give life to my mortal body by this same Spirit living within me (Romans 8:11). Thank you for your love and forgiveness!*

If you decided to believe in your heart and confess with your mouth, please know that all of Heaven is celebrating for you. Go find someone to celebrate with! Circumstances may still be the same, but you, my friend, are a new creation!

We have failed many people in the church today because we present life with Jesus as a silver platter. Everything served up for us now, no troubles or problems. When we really say yes to Jesus (the kind of yes where we would do anything for that person, give up anything and everything), we really begin transforming into the likeness of Jesus. If you have that yes in your heart, I encourage you to do as Jesus did:

- Get baptized in water.
- Set yourself apart for a time and fast (in church-speak we call that consecrating yourself).
- Ask God for the Holy Spirit to dwell in you and upon you every day.
- Recognize trials and temptations as God inviting you to walk a path where you receive the power of the Holy Spirit.

APPENDIX B

Resources

1) https://www.e-sword.net/
   This resource is available as an app and software. It's a comprehensive Bible study resource with commentaries, Strong's Greek and Hebrew, and parallel translations. Once downloaded, you do not have to have internet access to use.

2) https://biblehub.com/
   I use Bible Hub as a mobile Strong's concordance. It has a lot of information and features, and I love how easily you can navigate through their Strong's library.

3) https://bible.com

The YouVersion app is fantastic for having many versions of the Bible at your fingertips You can collaborate with friends, highlight verses, and make notes. There are lots of reading plans you can follow as well as prepared daily devotionals. A great resource for your mobile device.

Acknowledgements

First and foremost, I need to give thanks and full credit for this book to my friend and savior, Jesus Christ. He, along with Father God and the Holy Spirit, are the entire reason this book exists. "Yes, I am the vine; you are the branches. Those who remain in me, and I in them, will produce much fruit. *For apart from me you can do nothing*" (John 15:5).[1] Let this be much fruit for you, My God!

I would like to honor my husband, Shawn. Without him, this book would not be here. He took care of our precious children while I went away in the evenings to write. He developed a wonderful writing schedule and plan for me to follow and pushed me when I wanted to quit. His support during this process has been crucial. I LOVE you Sweets and thank God for you every single day!

---

1. Emphasis added.

I'd also like to thank my dad for challenging my theology and for his continued support. If I set my heart to do it, he stands behind me every step. I love you, Dad. I pray this book brings honor to you! Many of our discussions helped me while writing this book, and for that I say, "Thank you!"

Next, I want to thank and honor my spiritual parents and friends, Cherian and Sheeba. Their marriage as well as their walk has been a blessing to our family. When I was at my lowest point, I knew they were praying for me. Your discipleship is like no other. I love you all! Thank you for having an unusually intimate relationship with Jesus! I still want to be like you when I grow up.

Thank you, Thomas and Anna Thibeault! Your pursuit of publishing and your encouragement were key. Your love and continued support of me as well as your own success with publishing kept me going when I wanted to quit. I want to honor you both here. You are very special to me!

NOW IT'S YOUR TURN

Discover the EXACT 3-step blueprint you need to become
a bestselling author in 3 months.

Self-Publishing School helped me, and now I want them to help you with this FREE WEBINAR!

Even if you're busy, bad at writing, or don't know where to start,
you CAN write a bestseller.

With tools and experience across a variety of niches and professions,
Self-Publishing School is the only resource you need to take your book to the finish line!

DON'T WAIT

Watch this FREE WEBINAR now, and
Say "YES" to becoming a bestseller:

https://self-publishingschool.com/
Click on "Join Our Free Training"

About the Author

Tiffany is wife to her high school sweetheart, and mother to their three boys. After a series of events from teaching music to financial planning, she became a stay at home mom who loved to journal and write. Tiffany launched the blog, Letters to God, in 2018. As a result of the feedback, she decided to write this book. Tiffany is currently teaching this book as an introductory course for Pastoral students in Uganda through Manna Bible Institute and Rosewood Apostolic Center.

Can You Help?

Thank You For Reading My Book!

I really appreciate all of your feedback, and I love hearing what you have to say.

I need your input to make the next version of this book and my future books better.

Please leave me an honest review on Amazon letting me know what you thought of the book.

Thanks so much!

Tiffany Downs

www.ingramcontent.com/pod-product-compliance
Lightning Source LLC
Chambersburg PA
CBHW020908090426
42736CB00008B/535